MW01012360

Copyright © 1986 by Friendly Press, Inc.
All rights reserved under International and Pan-American Copyright Conventions.
Published by Friendly Press, Inc.,
401 Park Avenue South, New York City, 10016, United States of America.
Designed by Marty Goldstein.
Printed in Italy by Arnoldo Mondadori Editore Verona.

All the photographs in this book were enlarged in Witold Nowak's studio in Warsaw.
The authors are very grateful to Mr. Nowak
for his professional help and friendly cooperation throughout the project.

Photographs of Ms. Niezabitowska and Mr. Tomaszewski by Witold Nowak.
All other photographs © 1986 Tomasz Tomaszewski.

Library of Congress Cataloging-in Publication Data

Niezabitowska, Małgorzata
Remnants: the last Jews of Poland.

1. Jews—Poland. 2. Holocaust survivors—Poland.
3. Poland—Ethnic relations. I. Tomaszewski, Tomasz.
II. Title.
DS135.P6N49 1986 943.8'004924 86-1468
ISBN 0-914919-05-9

Written by
Małgorzata Niezabitowska

Photographed by
Tomasz Tomaszewski

Translated from the Polish by
William Brand and Hanna Dobosiewicz

We dedicate this book to the Polish Jews.
To those we came to know during the five years of our work,
to those who became our friends,
and also to those whom we never managed to meet—
in the hope that nevertheless and despite everything they are not the last.

Contents

Szczecin
Włocławek
Rembertów
Warsaw
Si
POLAND
Baniocha
Łaskarzew
Łódź
EAST
GERMANY
Legnica
Wrocław
Wałbrzych
Gliwice
Katowice
Kraków
Wadowice
CZECHOSLOVAKIA

Wilno
Białystok
iędzyrzec
Podl.
Włodowa
artów
blin
Chełm
Zamość
Biłgoraj
Lwów
U. S. S. R.

CENTRAL EUROPE

NETH
BELG
LUX
FRANCE
WEST GERMANY
EAST GERMANY
POLAND
U. S. S. R.
CZECH
SWITZ
AUSTRIA
HUNGARY
ROMANIA
ITALY
YUGOSLAVIA
BULGARIA

© FRIENDLY PRESS INC. 1986.

INTRODUCTION

WHY?

In 1800 three quarters of all the Jews in the world lived in Poland. In 1939 the three and a half million Polish Jews formed the second-largest diaspora. In 1980 about five thousand of them were left, the remnants.

It is they, the last Polish Jews, who are the heroes of our book.

Who are you looking for? Why are you doing this? These questions followed us through five years of work. They were posed by Jews, they were posed by Poles, and their mutual dislike, ignorance, and suspicion reflected as in a crazed mirror the whole tragic knot of Polish-Jewish destinies.

Of all the countries in the world it was Poland that first and for a long time represented—as the Jews themselves defined it—a paradise for Jews. But later, during the Second World War, it became a hell.

Poland was a paradise because for nine centuries there were no pogroms, and Jews who had been disinherited and persecuted elsewhere found secure asylum in Poland, and long possessed an autonomy that was close to sovereignty. This bore fruit in a great flourishing of civilization and spirit. Here arose one of the most powerful currents of Jewish religion, Chassidism; here giants of literature, thinkers, reformers, scholars, and politicians grew up and worked.

Poland was a hell because this is the land of the Holocaust, a cursed place marked with the stigma of crime. And even though that crime was planned and carried out by the Germans, its shadow fell upon the country and the people who were its witnesses and, what is worse, who did not always sympathize.

For these two reasons, Poland is so important to all the Jews who presently reside in Israel, the U.S., South America or Western Europe. Those among them who are seeking their roots and those who feel a moral obligation to honor the memory of their nation's martyrs must equally turn toward Poland.

And Jews still live in this Poland, even if nothing is known about them. History, after all, came to a standstill at the annihilation. It is completely understandable that thousands of reports, books, documents, and memoirs are dedicated to it. It is difficult to understand, on the other hand, why there is almost no interest at all in what remains of the splendidly exuberant and colorful world of the Polish Jews.

During the forty years since the war, only very dramatic events like the Kielce pogrom or the mass emigration of 1968 have drawn the world's attention to Polish Jews. Then they are spoken of loudly and at length both in Poland and beyond its borders, with totally different versions of events often being presented. And the rest is covered in silence. Yet something is still there. And even if it is only the last chapter in the nearly thousand-year-long history of the Polish Jews, it must be recorded.

We have decided to break this silence. And again the question arises: Why? Why the two of us, non-Jews, who were born after the war and for the next thirty years of our lives never saw a Jew, except for completely assimilated ones, with our own eyes?

One of our American friends once said, "This is the remnants describing the remnants." There is something to this. Both Tomasz and I, from family tradition rather than from date of birth, belong to a world that has vanished like the world of the Polish Jews, even if the motivation and the manner were different.

The Polish nobility and the intelligentsia that derive from it were swept away by the new system, and the values they represented were anathematized. They survived only among a narrow group of intellectuals and came to life in the times of Solidarity, which embraced the better part of the spiritual achievements of old Poland. But Solidarity lost and, as hard to accept as this fact may be, it too is receding into history and the task remaining for us, its former activists, is to watch over the legend.

My mother died very young. I was brought up by a grandmother from the Lwów region, where the family possessed land and an old, wooden manor house. After 1945 these environs, like more than one third of Poland's territory, were annexed to the USSR. Nothing was saved from the estate. There remained only tales of the "good old times." That was my entire inheritance.

Jews, the heroes of many of these stories, were an important part of it: the grain merchant Bergson, almost a member of the family; Zylberstein, in whose shop in a small border town one could buy all the confections of the East, southern fruits, and local delicacies throughout the year; Doctor Lewicki, who saved my father, a ten-year-old boy, from a violent attack of whooping cough; and the village tailors, shoemakers, and tanners, and the friends among the Lwów intelligentsia: lawyers, professors, journalists.

It was therefore plain to me that Jews, even if they were often separate and exotic, constituted a part of Poland and were as natural a part of its landscape as the towheaded boy following the plow. Yet when I grew up and began to look around carefully, there were no more Jews. Neither was my grandmother there, and her stories remained unfinished. For years she had only mentioned to me that during the war a Jewish family had been concealed in a special niche behind a wardrobe in her mother's house. When I wanted to know more, she would say, "I will tell you someday. These are tragic matters." And so I never came to know the second part of the fate of her former friends and acquaintances.

Of course, I knew about the destruction. There were ghettos and then there were death camps. The Germans murdered Jews, but then they also murdered Poles. Is such an effective amputation possible, then, that of three and a half million people and their powerful, varied world, nothing at all remains? A black hole...

And at the same time we have been frightened and are still frightened in Poland by the specter of the Jew. This has gone on for forty years. Whenever the situation in the country becomes really difficult, official propaganda or whispered gossip points to the victim. Jews are to blame for everything. As the leading Party activists, it was *they* who introduced the Stalinist terror, and as officers of the security apparatus *they* who carried it out in practice. It was *they* who led the students in demonstrations against state censorship in March 1968. Finally, it was *they* who as advisers to Solidarity manipulated Lech Walesa and the whole ten-million-strong movement.

So how is it, really? What remains of the great and exuberant Jewish civilization? Do Polish Jews still exist? And what does that mean?

No one could answer these questions for me. So I decided to look into it myself.

When I began, I never dreamed of how difficult it would turn out to be. Above all because taking up such a painful and complex subject required me to begin with myself: to overcome my own ignorance as well as my often unconscious presuppositions and stereotypes not only about both Jews and Poles but also about their mutual relations.

It was difficult because it also meant—and this is the reverse side of the same problem—overcoming the mistrust of many Jews still living in Poland and gaining acceptance in the closed circles where a *goy* is always an outsider and every Pole is an anti-Semite.

Neither Tomasz nor I is an anti-Semite or, for that matter, a philo-Semite. We are normal. Or at least we try to be. And we managed to convince many of the people we met of this. Otherwise, this book would have been impossible. The work on it lasted five years. During this time we traveled all over Poland looking for various Jewish communities as well as for individual people who were often the last Jews in their cities or towns. We took part in their daily life, in family and religious celebrations, in cultural and community events. The material piled up: more than seven thousand pictures and many hundreds of pages of text, which could best be defined as a history of absence.

Of the more than three and a half million Polish Jews, about five thousand are left. They are mostly old, lonely, ill people. The average age of the members of the Jewish communities is seventy. There are no children or young people: there is no middle generation. The fates of the majority of these people have been both unusual and astoundingly varied. But they all share the consciousness that something is irrevocably coming to an end, which gives their lives a tragic dimension. "We are definitely the last," we heard more than once, and also from the very few young. "Jews as a community, or even a mini-community, will no longer exist in Poland. We are on the way out."

The fact that it is we who are the witnesses of the end of a long epoch became an additional encouragement and also a moral obligation to describe and document it as well as we could. This was not easy for one more reason, this time rather more mundane: the lack of money. This is not the place to make a reckoning of how much we spent on traveling all over the country, on hotels, film, developing, and many other things. In any case it cost much more than we had. And because we financed ourselves almost to the very end, we often had to interrupt our work to make money to go on.

This occasioned many inconvenient and at times even dramatic moments, but it had one advantage: it gave us independence. No sponsor imposed his views on us, and no official patron censored us. Similarly, in the last stage when we signed the contract with Friendly Press that enabled us finally to bring the work to a conclusion, our publishers Marty Goldstein, Stuart Waldman,and Peggy Flaum exerted no pressure on us. Their friendly support, remarks,and advice gave us only courage and, at the same time, allowed us an indispensable critical distance toward our own work. For this we are very grateful.

Despite these obstacles and difficulties—or perhaps thanks to overcoming them—work on this book has given us much in a deeply personal sense, much more than we expected. We have gained several devoted friends, learned a great deal, and lost something of our arrogance and pride in exchange for a greater tolerance of others and their individuality, even when that individuality is sometimes annoying. We learned to speak forthrightly about matters that we previously had preferred to push aside. We also managed more than once to bring joy to people.

If we have managed to convey any of this here—and this is our great desire—it will perhaps do some good and become a step on the difficult road to reconciliation between Jews and Poles.

A unique sight in Poland: a Jewish mother with a small child. There are few children, few young people, and even the middle-aged are an exception.

Leja Szmidt, 92, in her home in
the village of Baniocha.
She and her large family ran a bakery
that supplied the whole local area before the war.
Her family perished during the war.
Other relatives emigrated. Leja lives entirely alone.
Her Polish neighbors help her.

Preceding page:
The Auschwitz-Birkenau death camp,
where more than four million people were gassed,
shot, hanged, or tortured to death.
The vast majority were Jews.

Feniks

C H A P T E R O N E

L U B L I N : I N S E A R C H O F A M I N Y A N

The last rabbi
migrated from Poland
ifteen years ago.
rom that time on,
rayers have been led
n particular cities
y devout lay people.
n Warsaw,
Mojżesz Szapiro
s such a man.

Lublin, the "Jewish Oxford," was famous throughout Europe for talmudic and cabbalistic learning. It was the second largest center of printing in the Hebrew language on Polish soil. The first *Yeshiva* in Poland was established here in 1515. Four hundred years later, the Talmudic School was to become the crowning glory of these traditions. Finished in 1930, active for only nine years before the Second World War broke out, it nevertheless educated many illustrious men. Its students went on to become the chief rabbis of Jerusalem and Tel Aviv.

In 1939 there were forty thousand Jews living in Lublin. The Germans confined all of them to the ghetto. Part of this population was murdered on the spot, and part was transported to the camps and exterminated there.

The Talmudic School building, known as the House of Peretz, survived the war. After the liberation it became a rallying point for most Jews. The Central Committee of Polish Jews was established there, a rabbinate was instituted, schools and cafeterias were organized. Transports from the depths of the Soviet Union arrived in Lublin. They carried tens of thousands of Polish Jews who had escaped eastwards from the Germans. Lublin also attracted those who had survived in the camps and in hiding places in Poland. They obtained aid and information at the House of Peretz. From there they set out for their new places of settlement, in Poland and in Palestine. Around a thousand remained behind.

Thirty-eight years later I have come to Lublin to find ten.

Is there still a *minyan* in Lublin? Nobody in Warsaw can answer that question for me. So I have decided to find out for myself.

The doors of the prayer house are closed and secured with two padlocks. Matys Zoberman, the *shammes* and thus the leader of the Lublin Jewish community, opens them with some difficulty. Zoberman is old and ailing, and these are serious padlocks, rusty and seldom used. The congregation gathers here for prayers on only the most important holidays. "*Rosh Hashanah, Yom Kippur, Simchat Torah, Pesach, Shavuot*"— he counts them off on his fingers as he lets me in.

The room is vast and almost bare: an old coat rack on one wall, benches falling apart along the other one. It takes me a moment to pick out the small pulpit, covered with faded material, near the window. A Star of David is embroidered at the top. Nearby stands a long simple table with shelves full of books behind it. There are many of them, and some have beautiful, richly imprinted bindings, but they lie in disorder, jumbled against each other, dusty. On the other side of the pulpit stands a plain, crooked cabinet. "That is *Aron Kodesh*, the sacred repository," Zoberman explains to me. "We have two *Torahs*."

Matys Zoberman lives in Lubartow, twenty-five kilometers from Lublin. Before the war it was a Jewish town, but now only he is left, the last one. He lives in the house of a cousin who went to America thirty-some years ago. They set out together on that journey, the two of them, the only survivors of an enormous, widely branched family. That was 1946. The way led through Germany. There they landed, like most Jewish emigres, in a refugee camp. They would have to wait there several months for transit visas to Palestine or the U.S. But Matys could not endure being behind the wires.

Barely a year earlier he had returned to Poland from Buchenwald, where he had been at the end of the war. Before that he had passed through many other camps. He had worked in quarries, in mines, and in ammunition factories. He had seen tens of thousands of Jews go to their deaths. So he was in no condition to live in a barracks, sleep on a plank, and look at guards with automatic rifles again. Not even if they had no ill intentions toward him.

He went back to Lubartow. Poles had already occupied his cousin's house. They made a small room available. He still lives in it. He had a horse and a cart. He hired himself out on odd jobs. He carted sand and stone. Later, when his health began to fail, he sold everything. He subsists on a pension.

Three years ago, after the death of the previous president, he was elected head of the Jewish community. He did not want the job. "I'm a simple man, modest," he explains with an embarrassed smile. "But they asked and insisted. 'You don't have anything else to do,' they said, 'or any family.' So I accepted. Although, you know, it's given me nothing but troubles."

The building in which the prayer house is located is very old and dilapidated. Once it all belonged to the community. Then tenants moved in upstairs. They were primitive people, perhaps malicious. They smashed their toilet, and excrement leaked down the walls. Zoberman shows me a place in the corner. The wall is still damp. The paint and plaster have peeled off over the spot. For a long time there was also a hole in the roof of the building. Water from rain and melting snow seeped down through two floors, making matters worse. Half the ceiling rotted. It took the municipal authorities two years to send a repair crew. They fixed it, and now it is in order. I look where he is pointing, at a rough bulge in the ceiling and a broad gray-brown spot.

"There's no money, there's no strength, there are no people..." The old man shakes his head in resignation.

"But once?" I ask.

"Ah, once..." His face brightens for a moment. "Fifteen or so years back there were twenty or thirty of us for prayers. We came every Saturday. There was a kosher cafeteria open, and Jews lived in the rooms across the hall. Then they left, they died. There were fewer and fewer of us, fewer...we dwindled until there was nothing left to dwindle."

"How many of you are there today?"

"A handful."

"But do you still have a *minyan* for prayers?"

"For the important holidays, everybody comes. They come from other places—from Włodowa, from Łuków, from Siedlce. And so a *minyan* somehow gathers."

"Who belongs to your *minyan*?"

Zoberman, who has been pleasant, even warm until now, suddenly stiffens. "Oh, that I can't say."

"Why not?" I ask, surprised.

"I would rather not name names."

"But Mr. Zoberman, you are the leader of a religious congregation that functions officially. What you do is in accordance with the law."

The old man looks at me in silence for a moment.

Then he says harshly, "I won't tell you. You can find them on your own."

The Lublin prayer ho
Sitting at the table is Matys Zoberm

The corridor of the apartment occupied by several families is cluttered to the ceiling. I pick my way among tubs of freshly washed linens. At the end of the corridor is a shabby door. The umbrella maker lives here, the second member of the Lublin *minyan* after the *shammes.* A woman greets me with a smile and leads me to her husband. When I appear, the old man gets up from the couch. He has a strange face, exotic and striking despite its undeniable ugliness. Everything seems too big, too expressive—his nose, his swollen eyes, his enormous mouth. He is wearing a nylon *yarmulka.* This is a big room, with tapestries hung Eastern-style on the wall; a television is playing in the corner. We sit around the table.

At first the man does not exactly understand why I have come, but when it sinks in, he reacts violently. "Nothing's going to come of this! I won't go for it!" His petite, delicate wife tries to mediate and she gets a scolding: "Quiet, mother!"

"And the fact that I say no, a completely decisive no, ought to be enough for you, Miss. Go and make an article out of that. You journalists know just how to do it," he says sarcastically. It does not help that I tell him that I have been gathering material about present-day Polish Jews, as straightforwardly and honestly as I know how, for a long time. "There was already one of them here, that wanted to shoot a film about me. I'm no monkey to be put on display."

"And do you know *The Self-Defense of the Republic*?" he asks, looking at me carefully.

"No, but I suppose it's something on the order of *The Bastion*."*

***Self-Defense of the Republic* and *The Bastion*—
Ephemeral, nationalistic and anti-semitic broadsheets that appeared irregularly and in small printings beyond the reach of the censor in 1981.

"What's that?" He is interested and for the first time listens to me attentively. I tell him how, before the introduction of martial law, I had wanted to write an article on anti-Semitism after coming across that bulletin. Then came December 13 and the subject was again officially taboo. I mention my *Solidarity Weekly** article, "The Cuckoo's Egg," about the beginnings of the openly anti-Semitic Grunwald Association. "You wrote it, Miss? Oh, yes, I read that..." For a moment it seems that he is softening and coming out of his shell, but then he catches himself. "I don't believe you and you don't believe me."

Saddened, I protest. This man with a bitter and mocking exterior is, for me, an unexpected discovery from the old Jewish world. A man with a modest occupation, simple, not wealthy, and yet respected for his wisdom and knowledge. My host enjoys demonstrating his knowledge. I am examined on the New Testament, the Decalogue, and the Hammurabic Code. In return, I ask for a couple of clarifications. He renders them willingly. I listen to a lengthy discourse on impure spirits and then to a detailed description of the celebration of *Simchat Torah.*

Unexpectedly the man pulls a postcard from his wallet. He orders me to read it. I do so with great difficulty because the card is in two halves; it is old and worn out. The postmark reads 1966. The address is my host's. Two nuns thank him for his help and express their warmest wishes on the occasion of *Pesach*, which, "as we have learned, your community celebrates solemnly."

When I have deciphered this proof of friendliness that he has carried next to his heart for almost twenty years, the old man says

* *Solidarity Weekly*—The official Solidarity weekly paper, the only one of its kind in the country, published in the very large—by Polish standards—press run of half a million copies. It was closed when martial law was declared on December 13, 1981.

with satisfaction, "You see!" But I have seen, I have seen all along—only how, my God, do you break through when the lack of trust is insurmountable? "Leave my corpse in peace," he says, attacking me again. "You are young. Write about the living." In reply I speak of a moral imperative that he, as a moralist, ought particularly to understand.

"So what do you want to write?"

"The truth."

"The truth?" He is scoffing again. "But there is no truth, there are only varying degrees of lies."

"Is that how a devout Jew talks?"

My host smiles unexpectedly. "You've got me there, Miss... Yes, yes, truth exists because God exists."

I sit there for a long time more, put off by the brutality of his expressions and arrested just as violently at every attempt to say good-bye and leave.

"What are you really looking for?"

"For people who feel that they are Jews," I answer, meeting his hypersensitivity as delicately as I can.

But this is precisely what angers him. "Feel, crap! What's wrong with you? 'Feel you're a Pole, feel you're a Jew.' One is a Pole and one is a Jew."

"All right, only—who is a Jew?"

"A Jew is somebody who believes in *Yahweh*," he answers with absolute certainty, forgetting in his excitement that it is forbidden to utter the name of God.

Marian Adler, the president of the Lublin Jewish Social-Cultural Association (JSCA)*, does not believe in *Yahweh*. He lost his faith as a young man, even though every one of the seven thousand Jews in his hometown of Biłgoraj was religious; some more, some less, but everyone observed tradition. His generation, which grew up in the two decades between the wars, was the first in which a significant number of the young stopped being religious. Some turned toward communism, and others assimilated and became Polish.

Adler joined the Communist Party of Poland. In that region the communists—Jews, Poles, and Ukrainians—"did their work" together. They distributed underground literature, agitated, formed trade unions or organized cells in the existing ones. "We kept the police busy," he recalls with satisfaction. He was arrested for communist activity and spent three years in prison.

"Is it true that politicals had it better?" I ask.

"Yes, we had our privileges, but a lot depended on the prison."

"Were you in many of them?"

"They shipped our fighters all over the country."

"And you were one of them?"

Marian Adler, handsome and blue-eyed and called *shabbes goy* by his friends in the JSCA because of his "Aryan" looks, smiles. "I was one of them and I saw quite a few things."

"There is a widely-held belief that the majority of the members of the Communist Party of Poland were Jews."

"There were a lot of Jews. I don't know if they were a majority, but

*Jewish Social-Cultural Association (JSCA)—
A government-supported organization charged with developing secular Jewish culture in Poland. Because of its communist orientation and anti-religious stance, a large number of Polish Jews distance themselves from it. It has branches in fourteen cities.

the ones in prison were almost all Jews. At least the ones I ran into."

"What do you see as the reason for such widespread Jewish participation in the communist movement?"

"The reason was simple. Jews were discriminated against. Mostly de facto, but sometimes officially too—after all, there were the ghetto benches* in the universities. Anti-Semitism was on the increase. 'Jews to Palestine'—you heard that a lot. So we supposed that socialism would be our salvation."

"Soviet-style communism?"

"Yes. The Soviet Union was the ideal," he says with sad irony. "A couple of people from Biłgoraj went there for training and never came back. And we envied them!"

"Later you ended up in the Soviet Union."

"At the beginning of the war I fled to the USSR. I was arrested there by the NKVD and transported to the far north, to Archangelsk. I was in a labor camp and the conditions were terrible. I was freed in the amnesty after Stalin's settlement with the Polish government in London. I wanted to join the Polish army, but I was so sick and exhausted that I didn't make it."

"When did you return to Poland?"

"In 1944. Like most of those who came back, I landed in Lublin. I met old friends, I started to work in the Jewish Committee, and I stayed. Those were hard times, but a lot of good was accomplished. There were still several hundred thousand Polish Jews; their presence was felt, and various institutions were active. There was life in it. In 1947 we organized

*Ghetto benches—In the thirties, as a result of growing anti-Semitism, Jews were forced to sit at separate benches in many Polish universities.

a congress of Jews in Lublin. Hundreds of them came, maybe more. Rumors spread around town that they were coming to take back their homes, and there was a panic."

"I understand that the Jews of Lublin were scattered around the country partly because those homes had been occupied."

Adler is silent for a moment, and then he begins to speak slowly and deliberately. "Yes. It was a complicated problem. After the liquidation of the ghetto, part of the property was taken over by the Germans and part was sold to Poles. After the war so many people turned up here and were fighting for apartments, and everybody was living jammed together, so where could they put those Jews? I knew a Jew who had owned a beautiful apartment house before the war, and afterward he lived with his concierge until he moved to the Recovered Lands.* There was a lot of room there."

"Yet a certain group stayed."

"Of course. Some who were there before the war and some who were new to the city, like me."

"What happened to them?"

"They were carried away by successive emigrations. Until sixty-eight** our club was full. We had a cafe, a youth group, a rock group, dance evenings. All the young left. There are only a few of the old remaining. We meet sometimes, ten or twelve people. We rented our space to the Lawyer's Council because we didn't need all that room, and we gave the musical instruments to an orphanage. Sometimes there are lectures; once in a while some actor comes... We also try to help the

*Recovered Lands—After the Second World War, Poland lost almost half its territory to the Soviet Union. This land was called "recovered" because Poland claimed a historical right to part of it.

**1968—A date and a symbol, also referred to as "March '68."
Student demonstrations became the pretext for an anti-Semitic campaign organized and manipulated by the authorities. Many Jews were fired from their jobs. As a result, approximately twenty-five thousand of them emigrated, the final great emigration of Jews from Poland. The date is regarded as one of the watersheds in postwar Polish history.

sick and the lonely. And that's about it."

"What do you think about communism now?"

"You know, it is a beautiful idea. Noble. But it depends on who carries it out."

"And how do you see your role in its creation?"

"They say here that the Jews gave Poland communism and then escaped to Israel themselves. Well, I haven't left, at least."

"Why not?"

"I am alone. I have nowhere to go."

Marian Adler at his home.

The second Jewish communist in town is Edward Ungier. He has known Adler since their prewar Party activism; they are still friends, and they go to the prayer house together. "We don't believe," Ungier says, "but we go so that there can be ten and they can pray. They need to be supported somehow, don't they?"

Years ago, when there were a lot of Jews in town and they all had more strength and enthusiasm and better health, those from the Jewish Social-Cultural Association and those from the religious community did not get along with one another. Some were even hostile. The devout called the Party members traitors and *shkotzim*. The communists called the faithful ignorant and backward. Today, when there are so few of them left, and age, loneliness, and sickness are affecting them all equally, the conflicts of bygone years seem less relevant. Only rarely in a conversation will a weak echo of the old passions surface.

Edward Ungier, too, feels old, sick, and lonely. In his youth he was athletic. He threw two-hundred-pound sacks on his back, worked all day without any fatigue, and if you mention food... His mother could not keep up, especially since there were nine children at home and his father, a tailor, brought home barely enough to make ends meet.

He lost his strength in the Soviet Union. "I was a wreck when I got back from there," he says. Five years of war, camps, and hunger did the job. He had scurvy and insomnia, and his nerves were shot. He never really felt well again; now he suffers from every possible infirmity: diabetes, prostate, kidney, and circulatory failure. But the worst torments are the moral ones.

"During the war the only thing I wondered about was whether I would ever be lucky enough to see a loaf of bread lying on the table, slice it, and eat it in peace. Oy, I thought then. I may never live to see the day. So when I survived and returned to Poland, all I wanted was peace. But that was not given to me, either."

"Why not?"

"Because I was a Jew."

"You were made to feel this?"

"Here there's an anti-Semitism in white gloves. As if there isn't any. But there is."

"How does it show itself?"

"When I arrived in 1945, my comrades in the Party at once took me aside and said, 'Edward, you're going to be a big shot here, a manager. We'll find you something right away.' But I didn't want it. I don't have the education, you see. So I went to work in an office. And it was good. I worked in peace until I retired. But it came out from time to time nevertheless."

"What?"

"Everybody else would win awards, but never me. They gave me a lower pension than I was entitled to. And so on. And in the end it would always come out: 'Because you're a Jew.' But the worst was with my children."

"You have a daughter and son."

"They both turned out well-educated, university graduates. 1968 was very hard on them. Seeing that my wife is Polish, and in addition I did not practice religion, the children were brought up completely Polish. And then, in sixty-eight, my Jewishness was thrown in their faces. My son took it so hard that he nearly became an anti-Semite."

"How is that?"

"Everybody was talking about Jews then, and in various ways they jabbed at him. He would come home and fret over it and ask, 'Why Dad? Am I worse than everybody else?'"

"Your son emigrated after 1968?"

"No, no. I was just talking about that with Adler the other day. Where were our brains? We should have left back in 1946, after the Kielce pogrom.* Or in 1968 for sure. But Adler steered me wrong in 1968. 'Stay,' he said. 'We're not so bad off here. Let's see what happens next. They'll always let us out.' The years went by, and we kept on getting older and more feeble. And so now they'll let us out, that's for sure, but where is there anybody to take us in?"

"And yet your children are not in Poland."

"My daughter left first, in 1978. She settled in Canada, near Vancouver, along with her husband, a Pole. My son and his wife and their six-year-old daughter finally emigrated in 1981. Late, far too late. He was already pushing forty. Now both families are living in a little town on the Pacific. And it's hard for me here, so very hard, because I know that I will never see them again. That's terrible. Even in the hour of my death I will be completely alone. They cannot come here. I'm very ill and I have neither the strength nor the money to go on such a journey. And what do I have for the rest of my life? Letters and photographs."

*Kielce pogrom—Forty-two Jews were killed
and fifty wounded at a pogrom in Kielce on July 4, 1946.
The direct perpetrators were punished, but
the background of the crime has never been clarified.

The daughter of Szmulewicz the tailor did not leave. She lives in Lublin, just a few blocks away, but for Szmulewicz, the fifth member of the Lublin *minyan*, it would be better if she were not here at all. Two years ago she married a Pole: her father cursed her and turned her out of his home.

We are sitting in his tailor shop. It opens right onto the same street where, two hundred yards away, the Jewish community building stands. The premises are small and cluttered. Material, garments, and cuttings lie everywhere. Szloma Szmulewicz is a good tailor, very successful. The occupation, a traditional one among Polish Jews, was passed from father to son in his family. In him, the tradition has come to an end. Szmulewicz has only one child, the daughter who studied to become a teacher. "But instead of showing gratitude, such a shame she has become to me," he says. "She turned into the tragedy of my life."

A religious Jew, as he defines himself, Szmulewicz does not want to know anything about his daughter and does not even want to think about her. Yet he cannot speak about anything else. Endlessly, obsessively, he returns to the same theme: how they deceived him, how they failed him, how his own wife, a Jew to boot, helped them.

"But Mr. Szmulewicz," I manage to break in, "how else could it have turned out? Just who was your daughter supposed to marry?"

"A Jew."

"But there are no young unmarried Jewish men."

The tailor seems not to take this into consideration.

"She should have married a Jew," he repeats.

rd Ungier in his apartment.

"For that you would have had to take her to Israel or America."

"So we might have been able to go someday, but she didn't want to wait."

"Were you really planning a journey? Seriously?"

"Well, nothing really definite . . . But did that give her the right to marry a *goy*, a Pole?"

"Why not?"

"Because all Poles hate Jews."

"All Poles hate all Jews? Mr. Szmulewicz..."

The tailor, however, will not be reconciled. As we talk, the door opens every so often. Clients walk in for fittings, and friends to chat. The shop grows crowded, so I edge toward the exit. Right in front of the door I notice a large photograph hanging over the sewing machine: several laughing people sitting around a table on a terrace.

"What's the picture?" I ask.

"That's the forester's house where I hid during the war," Szmulewicz answers.

"And who are they? Jews?"

"Jews? What Jews? Those are the foresters, the Poles who saved my life."

Szloma Szmulewicz in his shop during a conversation with a customer.

As a woman, Zofia Grzesiak does not count among the *minyan*. Nevertheless, she alone, of all the Jews in Lublin, comes from a priestly family. Her father, Mordche Wolf Szwarcblat, a poor but very religious and respected man, was a *koyen* and served as a cantor. His daughter Nechume became Zofia one tragic day in 1941 when the well-disposed community secretary warned her and her mother that they were both to be ordered to Zabludow. That meant death. There was not even a ghetto there; neither were there transports to the camps. When Jews arrived in Zabludow they dug graves for themselves. Then they were all killed. So Mrs. Buksztel, the wife of a bank clerk, gave Nechume her daughter's high school diploma. From that moment on she became Zofia Gresiak, née Buksztel, born 1921, parents' names...well, even now when she is asked her parents' names in an office somewhere Zofia has to grit her teeth to avoid saying "Mordche and Rejza"; she constantly forgets the official data and ends up handing them her identity booklet. Let them read it themselves.

That day, transformed into an Aryan by a flimsy piece of paper, she buried everything that could give her away. She threw the photographs of her loved ones, letters, family documents, and old Hebrew and Yiddish books and papers into the hole she had scooped out. She gave the only valuable possession she had—a gold watch decorated with pearls, her mother's wedding present—to the woman who had warned her. In exchange she got a head start, time enough to cover sixty miles. She had nothing left, only images and memories of the people to whom she had been born and who had raised her.

Ukrainians, Jews, and Poles had lived together in her native village for centuries. In 1945 that village fell within the borders of the Soviet Union. Its people had been killed or scattered to the winds. Many years later, living in Lublin, Zofia-Nechume began going back to the lives of those people and that town, a world that no longer existed. She started writing her stories and novels.

In her small apartment I am examining a cabinet full of papers. They lie in confusion, some faded and some in tatters. Not a single page has ever been published or submitted anywhere. No one beyond her immediate family—her husband and her daughter—knows that Zofia has been writing for more than twenty years. According to her husband, she has written seventeen thousand pages. He, a boy from the same village, the son of the blacksmith who lived across the road, is her first, faithful, enthusiastic reader.

"I love my wife's writing," he says. "Her work is real. I knew all those people."

Zofia-Nechume herself, today a delicate, quiet, nervous woman in her seventies, speaks of her writing with great uncertainty. She is ashamed of her lack of education. She did not finish even the third grade in the *cheder* and she never went to school afterward. She repeats this over and over during our long conversation, and each time it sounds like a plea for forgiveness.

"My downfall was that my husband was a craftsman of the old school and he never imagined not supporting his wife. If I had gone to work I would have finished school and made something of myself. And instead I spent my whole life as a scullery maid, a washerwoman, a nanny, a mother, a grandmother—but never myself. My husband understands now, because when you come down to it, I was a girl with abilities."

After considerable resistance she decides to read one of her stories. I am astonished. I have been afraid that it will be mere scribbling, or at best exalted memoirs. Instead the story of Rejzka, who wanted desperately to find a husband, is quite good by any standards: dramatic construction, concise, striking descriptions, sharp dialogue. When I tell her this, Zofia looks more embarrassed than pleased.

"You have to publish it," I add.

Zofia reacts violently, as if she is terrified. "I'm not counting on anything. It never crossed my mind to have that published. I thought, maybe my grandson will know what to do with it, what to make of it, if he turns out to be wise."

She began to write in her native language, Yiddish, as a child. But the real beginning was a sleepless night twenty-five years ago. She got out of bed at four in the morning. If she had not found a pen and some paper, it might have turned out differently. But everything was there, so she sat down and tried to write a memoir and then, without knowing how, she was in the Urals where, during the 1917 revolution, her beautiful Aunt Sara, one of her mother's six sisters, found her husband, the owner of a large estate, in a beet field where he had been clubbed to death by the peasants. Half-mad with fear, she returned to the manor house. That same night she wrapped her baby daughter in gold chains and priceless jewelry under her blankets and escaped across the river in a small boat.

And she has been writing ever since that first story.

"I never know what I write," says Zofia. "I write because it writes itself for me. They themselves, my heroes, command me and guide me. But when I've written I don't even like to read it. And now I've got so much that I don't know what I have."

"You put it well when you said that the writing is a monument being built to those who died," adds her husband.

"I lead them along those roads that no longer exist."

"What was life like in a devout Jewish home?" I ask.

"To be a Jew was awfully difficult. The customs were severe, the laws were rigid—although when I think about it today I can see that many of the prescriptions were for health. Those wise men and doctors who laid down the rules back then thought: If the people are going to live in poverty, at least let them not be devoured by filth. So they enforced hygiene. At home we followed it all very precisely. Not only was the food kosher, but also the soap. There were separate dishes for the milk and meat dishes, and also separate washbasins and towels. In every door frame, of course, there was a *mezuzah*, a metal container with verses from the Holy Scripture written on parchment. During *Succoth* the sky must be visible overhead, so there was a special construction, ropes and a shaft, by which the roof was lifted. The table stood under this, and we ate supper looking at the stars. Mother ran the kitchen extremely rigorously. It was forbidden to eat fish without scales like eels, and no game: only homegrown chickens. For the *Shabbes* those chickens were taken to the *shochet*, two and a half miles from our village, and he performed the ritual slaughtering and checked that they weren't *trayf*. We baked *challah*, and the table was covered with a white tablecloth. Mother lighted the candles—two for the marriage and one for each child, but only up to seven. Then we ate, prayed, and sang songs.

"On Saturday mornings Daddy dressed for prayers. He recited the *Shir-ha-shirim*, the Song of Songs, and went to the prayer house. The women did not have to pray. Only on some great holidays. When Daddy came back from the prayer house, the *shabbes goy* came too. He carried candles around the rooms, lighted them, and took the dinner that had been cooked on Friday out of the oven, because we were not allowed to do anything. And father, a passionate smoker and a very good man, was angry the whole *Shabbes* because for twenty-four hours he was forbidden to put a cigarette to his lips. He could only, like all of us, sit and pray. That was absurd."

"Did you revolt?"

"That would be saying too much, but I asked questions, and Daddy didn't like smart-aleck questions. A lot of things got on my nerves, but there was also a lot that I loved."

"What, for example?"

"The holidays. Jewish holidays are beautiful and thrilling. If you take part in them, you cannot be indifferent."

"How did you, a girl from a religious family, manage to marry a *goy*?"

"I didn't manage. We were really together only after the war broke out. My father was no longer alive, and everything had stopped working the way it used to. Before that the only thing I'd accomplished was fighting off being married according to my parents' wishes."

"Whom had they chosen for you?"

"Marriages were contracted without love among the Jews. Matchmakers would come and establish the value of the dowry, from which they took a percentage, and they looked for an appropriate boy. And I didn't even have three hundred dollars."

"Why three hundred?"

"By custom, that was the smallest dowry. But even though I had no dowry, Joisef, the son of wealthy parents, wanted to marry me. They lived by usury and ran wool-carding machines and a vegetable oil mill. I hated him, he turned my stomach, and besides I loved Tadeusz. My torment lasted for two years. My parents kept insisting because it was an unheard-of opportunity, a rich boy wanting to marry a barefoot girl in rags. Joisef wanted to buy me. I didn't let him."

"Didn't your father like Tadeusz?"

"On the contrary, he liked him and valued him highly. For those times and that place he was well educated and well mannered, and besides he knew his craft inside out. My father would repeat, 'He is a *tzaddick*, but let him marry among his own kind.'"

"Even between two people of the same religion and customs, marriage is a difficult business. And you were a religious Jew and your husband was a Catholic and a Pole."

"It took sacrifices on both sides. We both had to renounce our faith, and if it hadn't been for the war we might have had to renounce our families as well. But the war and that great tragedy changed everything. My mother even lived with us. Tadeusz was truly a good son-in-law. He got kosher meat for her even at the worst of times."

"Were you already eating everything?"

"Yes, even though at first it made me very sick. Later, when my whole family had been killed and Tadeusz and I had to change our hiding place for the thirteenth time, it really didn't mean anything."

"Your husband went into hiding because of you?"

"At the beginning, yes, but afterward on account of himself. Most of the inhabitants of that region were Ukranians, and after 1942 the local bandits were killing all the Poles."

"And all the Jews."

"The Jews they turned over to the Germans. Poles sheltered us until it got to the point that a Jew could stay in hiding but a Pole could not. That was when we decided to report for work in Germany. After the war Jews who had survived would tell me, 'You were lucky. You had a good face.'* And in fact, nobody spotted me. They took us to Vienna along with our little daughter, and we waited out the end of the war there."

"And then you came to Lublin?"

"I was looking for my family, and I also wanted to get some kind of help, because we had nothing. But in that committee, in the House of Peretz, some clerk asked me in a rage, 'Why doesn't your child know Yiddish?' That hit me like a thunderbolt. I asked him, 'Where did you hide? That was her great fortune, that the little one didn't know Yiddish, that why she's alive.' I picked up my child and never returned there. We

*"Good face"—Popular term for un-Jewish, Aryan features which greatly facilitated the survival of Jews during the Second World War.

traveled to the Recovered Lands and one way or another we made it."

"Did you meet Jews there?"

"No, I lived only among Poles. I taught myself their customs, and often they did not know that I was a Jew."

"Did you hide it?"

"No. I am made up of two personalities. One is very proud, and the other is small and weak. But that proud self would not allow me to hide it. I did nothing wrong. I am a very honest person."

"Did you encounter any anti-Semitic reactions?"

"Of course not. After we returned to Lublin I subscribed for years to *Folks-Styme** and all the neighbors knew about it but none of them ever said anything nasty to me. My husband's family accepted me, and they are peasants, after all."

"Would you say that there is no anti-Semitism in Poland?"

"Well, there was that bad year 1968, wasn't there? Then I suffered such a shock that somehow the Jewish culture left me. From that time on it has been hard for me to write about Jews. Anti-Semitism? ... Well, you can look it up in the dictionary. It's always been there, it's there now, and it will be there in the future."

"Can a person like you, brought up in a religion that not only organized a person's whole life but also penetrated deeply into the personality, leave it all behind and uproot it all?"

"That's very difficult. You swim away from one bank, and you don't make it to the other side."

**Folks-Styme*—Semi-weekly JSCA publication in Yiddish with Polish sections. Currently the only Yiddish newspaper in Poland.

Zofia Grzesiak, with her husband, in the kitchen. She does most of her writing here.

Henryk Laden, the sixth member of the Lublin *minyan*, lives seventy miles to the north in the town of Siedlce. Laden's everyday dress is a semi-military jacket with three rows of ribbons and miniature medals pinned on the chest. Their originals completely cover half of the dress uniform jacket to which they are affixed. That jacket hangs in the closet, always ready to be put on. And Laden puts it on often, even if there is no holiday. His richly equipped apartment is full of mementos from the Second World War: pictures, photographs, military memorabilia of various kinds. The army was the great love of Laden's life—one that was not fully requited.

"I made history," he says, and he is not exaggerating much. Today every pupil learns about the First Kósciuszko Division, which was the beginning of today's army, and schoolchildren know its ballads, sung in faraway Russia by Poles and Polish Jews freshly liberated from Soviet penal camps. Henryk Laden, arrested and transported to Siberia at the beginning of the war, had four years of difficult residence in the USSR behind him. So as soon as he heard about the creation of a Polish army in the Soviet Union, he left the collective farm where he had spent the last few months. He arrived at Shelts on the Oka in May, 1943, among the first volunteers. He became a gunner on a cannon in the First Light Artillery Regiment. The equipment that they had then was at best modest: obsolete weapons, and horses, donkeys, and camels as transport. These not only carried personnel but also pulled cannons and ammunition.

Things did not change until the United States sent fourteen thousand vehicles and components for twice as many more to Moscow as aid to its ally. Then Laden's "historical role," as he calls it, began.

"We were in the middle of exercises," he recalls, "when the regimental commander along with a freshly assigned Russian officer, Captain Mayevsky, came to us. They read a proclamation and told us about those vehicles that had been sent to Moscow, and also said that somebody had to go and pick out something for our division. The commander asked who was a driver or automobile mechanic. Only two of us volunteered from the whole regiment because all the experts had left earlier with Anders' army.* So the two of us were supposed to do everything. That was a real job.

"First of all, we had to turn horse drivers into truckdrivers immediately. So I quickly created a driver education course. I chose a few dozen boys. The only problem was that I had to explain everything theoretically, because we didn't have even a single vehicle for training.

"Soon afterward I was sent to Moscow with Captain Mayevsky. When we arrived, it was a sight for sore eyes. I can see it to this day. Brand-new Studebakers, Jeeps, Chevrolets, Dodges, and Willyses stood there in rows: just take your pick and go. Never in his life had Mayevsky seen such a miracle, but to me it was like Poland before the war. After all, I had been a professional driver and cars were my passion, too. So I immediately began selecting: these for the cannon, these for cargo, and light models for communication. I explained everything in detail. The Russians were dumbstruck, because in those days none of them knew such things. I had to stay in Moscow and carry out requisitions for the whole army. I was also training drivers all the time, mostly Poles.

*Anders' army—A Polish army under General Anders was created in the USSR, made up of Poles transported into the depths of the Soviet Union and for the most part settled in camps there in 1939–41. After the worsening of Polish-Soviet relations it left the Soviet Union, reaching North Africa by way of Persia. It proceeded to fight alongside the western allies until the end of the war.

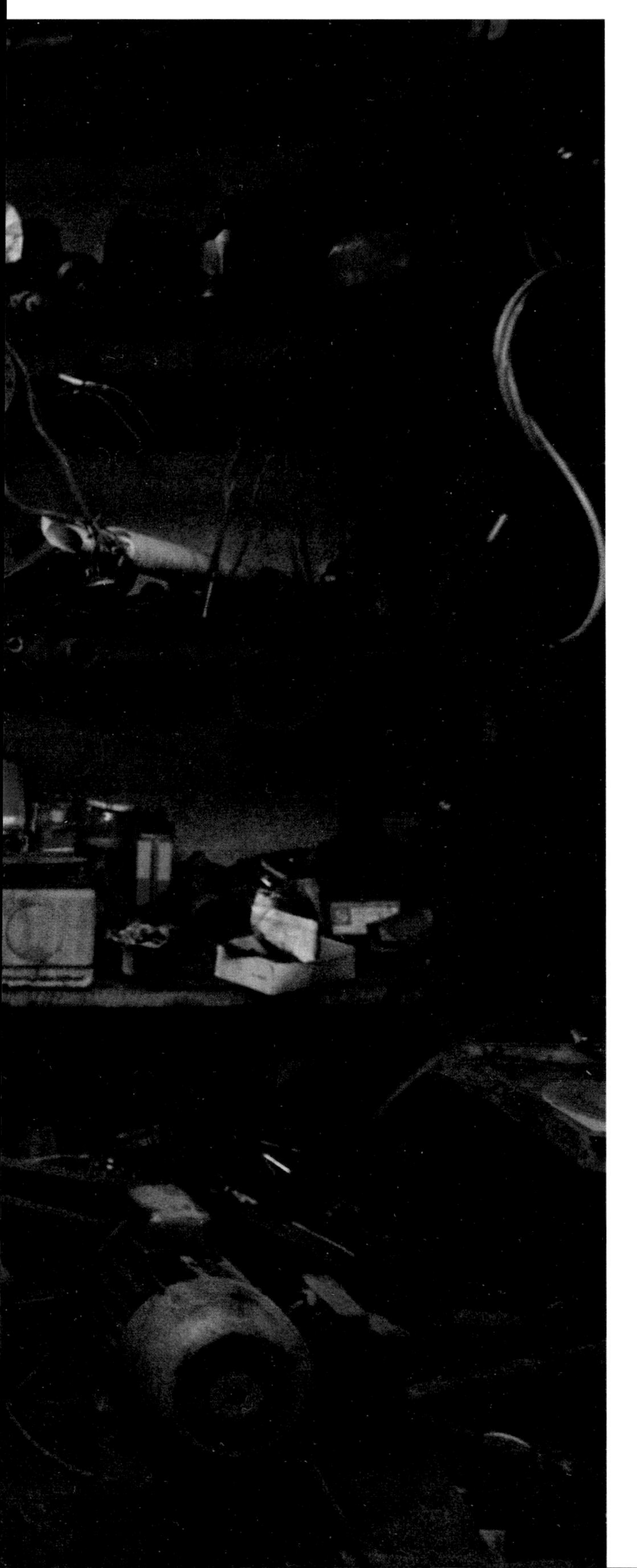

Later I went to the front with them in those vehicles."

Laden covered the whole operational route of the First Polish Army, from the famous initial battle at Lenino to Berlin, which they took in May, 1945. Over the space of these thousands of miles, Laden led "his" vehicles, trained personnel to service them, and created repair brigades. He also drove first in the order of attack before each battle in order to choose positions and dig in the vehicles "so the bombs wouldn't blow them out from under me." Laden tells me about the battles and the skirmishes and the victories and the setbacks for hours. To this day he is very proud of his division.

Henryk Laden, former Polish Army captain and a taxi driver for more than thirty years, in his garage.

"At Lenino the Russians had been stymied for many months and could not move the front, but in the course of twenty-four hours we pushed the Germans back five miles. Even though it was our baptism of fire and we had practically no experience. And that was really hell there. Six hundred cannon, countless *katyushas*, mortars. Every barrel was red-hot from firing. Heaven and earth trembled."

Several months later Laden was severely wounded. After being treated, he did not even want to take the leave that was due him. As soon as he walked out of the hospital, he took off to catch up with his regiment. He rejoined it and accompanied it across Polish soil right up to Berlin. There, standing below among the rubble of the devastated city, he watched as soldiers raised the Polish flag above the Brandenburg Gate. That symbolic gesture signifying the ultimate fall of the Third Reich was "the most beautiful moment in my life," he says today.

"Were there a lot of Jews in the First Army?" I inquire.

"Oh, yes, a lot. There were five of us from my little town near Lwów: Markus Lang, Pomeranz, Targielski, Reiser, and me. A list of Jewish soldiers from the First Division who were killed in action was published in a Jewish Historical Institute bulletin. There is a page and a half of names and another page and a half of those who were decorated. That showed that Jews aren't so full of fear, that they can fight just as well as others, sometimes better. Unfortunately, that part of the history of Polish Jews is little known."

"What were the relations between Polish and Jewish soldiers like?"

"In camp, correct, and at the front, very good. Shedding blood together unites. Besides, enemy bullets do not pick and choose—that was true equality."

"You served in the army until 1951?"

"That's right. After the war I went on fighting against reactionary bands. Afterward I was second in command of a regiment in the Biala Podlaska division. I led all the technical equipment of the Polish Army in the 1949 May Day parade. On the radio you could hear over and over, 'Laden and his vehicles . . .' "

"So why did you leave?"

"It was not entirely of my own accord. There were all sorts of shady goings-on in the regiment: things being sold under the counter, vehicles disappearing in midnight requisitions, and afterward there were nice profits to split. But I wouldn't take money, and I also didn't want to give them my vehicles. So my career came to an end. They even wanted to put me on trial on false charges, but I stood up to them and it didn't come off. In any case I had to get out. That was my recompense for all I'd done. Then . . . I settled in Siedlce, bought an old Volga, rebuilt it and made it into a taxi. It was the first taxi in town. I still drive, even though I'm seventy-eight now, and my taxi still has 'Number One' painted on the door."

"Did you marry?"

"My wife was Polish, but loved Jews more than some of our own do. We lived together for twenty-five years until she died, and such another one in this world does not exist. She was an angel. She even went to the synagogue with me, especially on *Yom Kippur.* She wanted to weep together with me for my family. There were nine of us: three brothers and six sisters. Before the war broke out there were thirty-six people in the immediate family. They all died. Young and old. So I have someone to say *kaddish* for."

"Mr. Laden, forty years have passed since the end of the war. Why do you still wear your decorations?"

"Out of sentiment. I well remember those days when I won them. Look here—this is the Lenino medal, this one is for taking Warsaw, for crossing the Oder, for capturing Berlin, for victory over the Germans ... This is the Battle Cross, and beside it the Silver Cross for Distinction in the Fields of Glory, another Silver Cross ...."

Laden shows them to me one by one, counting them off. Then he pauses, smiles, and adds completely unexpectedly, "But you know, it's all worth as much as a sucked egg."

"The most devout among us is Rafael Adar," one of the Lublin Jews confided. The Adars live in Włodowa, a small town smack on the Soviet border, fifty-five miles east of Lublin.

The little house stands on a quiet side street. Low, wooden, with a small veranda and a yard not much bigger than the veranda. An old, gray-haired woman is sitting on a bench near the door. She remains motionless, observing the street along which I am approaching her. When I come up to her and ask after the Adars, she beams and grasps my hand.

"That's me, child. I'm Sara Adar. Have you come especially to see us? Oy, that's good, that's good. Nobody visits old people. Come here, daughter, and let me give you a kiss."

Amazed and moved by such a reception, I bend to kiss the woman on the cheek and she raises herself and hugs me tight. We enter the house with our arms around each other. It is divided into one room and a kitchen. Sara moves back and forth trying to think of how to make me as comfortable as she can. She worries that she has nothing in the house and good-naturedly scolds me for arriving unannounced. She would have baked a cake and cooked a good dinner. Every so often she sits down in one of the chairs and breathes heavily. Her severe asthma makes quick movement impossible. After innumerable assurances on my part that I want nothing besides a cup of tea, we sit down together at the small table.

"Oh, Rafael will be so happy that you've come," she says, smiling. "We live here entirely alone. For whole months nobody comes to see us except the lady from Public Welfare. She cleans and cooks us dinner every day because we don't have the strength anymore."

"And friends, neighbors?" I ask.

"We left our friends behind in Lublin, where we lived for many years. Oh, they all crowded around me then. I was young and healthy. I cooked dinner for the whole Jewish community, dozens and dozens of people. And the neighbors? Good-hearted people, but they have their own lives. We are old Jews. The last Jews in town."

She recalls earlier times. Before the war there were so many Jews in Włodowa that it would take you days to enumerate them. When they walked the main street on Sunday afternoon there was such a crowd that they poked each other with their elbows as they passed. A hubbub, but happy. Yet on the *Shabbes* such a sudden total silence fell. Only dogs moved around outside the houses, candles shined in every window, the singing from the many synagogues carried on the peaceful air.

The old woman tells it so colorfully and vividly that I do not even hear her husband come into the room.

"Oh, Rafael," Sara cries as she gets up and leads her husband to me. "Look, dear, whom heaven has sent to us. Our daughter has come." He smiles, and we join hands in an embrace.

Rafael Adar is a short, slight man dressed in an old threadbare suit, with a felt hat on his head. The face under the hat is unusually soft, benevolent, and seems somewhat absent. We greet each other warmly, like old friends.

"I brought you the medicine," Rafael says and sets a big bag full of boxes and bottles on the table. "Please take the ones that the doctor prescribed now."

"Oy, that's healthy." Sara waves her hand, but she obediently begins swallowing the correct pills. "I've been so sick, and now I suffer like a condemned soul from this asthma and thyroid. And I love life so much. I don't want wealth, I've never insisted on that. All I want is to get through the day. And then one more...."

Sara shakes her gray head, and I have no difficulty imagining how she was once young and full of energy and ran through the fields in the nearby village of Hannia, and how she raced against her brothers to swim the Bug, the wide river bordering the family farm. She swam the river for the last time to escape to the Soviet side shortly after the Germans arrived.

When she returned after seven years, she had no parents, no family, no relatives. In Włodowa the Jews no longer went out for walks, and Friday had become just another day. All that remained was the land—seventy acres, which she first rented out to peasants and later turned over to the state in exchange for a pension.

Rafael has gone to the kitchen to make tea for himself. Sara watches him sadly.

"My Rafael isn't what he once was. A year ago he had a stroke and it paralyzed him. He's more or less recovered, but it changed him. His memory is going. It's happening slowly. And he used to know the whole *Torah* and half the *Talmud* by heart, and what *midrashes* he could tell! People would listen for hours."

Sara falls silent and bows her head. The old man stands in the doorway smiling gently at us.

"Rafael, sing something," Sara says, lively again. "Because you know, daughter, my Rafael is not a cantor, but when he opened his mouth to pray you didn't want to eat anything, not even on *Yom Kippur.* And we fast for twenty-four hours. We don't even take a drop of water to our lips."

"What should I sing, Sara?" asks Rafael, still smiling.

"*El male rachamim.* That makes my heart lighter." The old man is silent for a moment, as if he is concentrating. Then he begins to sing. "*El male rachamim*—Lord, full of mercy." The melody rises sharply. Then it falls and comes back again, dramatic and strong. Rafael stands in the middle of the room, hands upraised. When he finishes, he sinks exhausted onto the sofa. We sit in silence for a long while.

Then Sara turns to me. "And when they brought him to me, he was so skinny, miserable, and beat up. That was not long after the war. I had no one and he had no one. He had lost his whole family. His wife was pregnant... He had it good before the war. He was studying at the *Yeshiva* in Zamosc. He was studying Scripture and he didn't have a worry. His rich father-in-law was proud of his learned son-in-law and paid the bills. And so afterward, when he had lived through that nightmare, he was as lost as a child—even though he knew many things. He was a *shochet* like his father and grandfather. And I was looking for a friend for life, so it would be good. Acquaintances in Lublin found him and brought him here to me. We were introduced. I fed him a little, dressed him, and we went to a rabbi I knew in Legnica to get married. Oy, that was a story. Everything ready. I was alone in a room with the women when suddenly it hit me. No mother, no father, no sister, no brother. Strangers are going to lead me to the *chuppah.* What do I need such a wedding for? I don't want it! And I started to cry and scream. Nobody could calm me down. They coaxed and coaxed until they convinced me."

"But I see now that you don't regret it," I interject.

"How could I regret it?" Sara snorts. "He took me to Lublin. He was *shochet* there. He slaughtered and I cooked kosher dinners for the whole community. We lived in a room near the prayer house. It was a good life. Now, well, in our old age we returned to this little house and only on holidays do we travel back to our former haunts. What to do?"

When I leave their home a few hours later, they walk me to the street. We say long good-byes. It is somehow hard for me to leave. At the corner I turn around. The small wooden house is perfectly visible from there. On the bench by the door sit two old people. Sara is resting her head on Rafael's shoulder. They are silent, looking straight ahead at the empty street.

Sara and Rafael Ader in front of their house in Włodowa.

The cemetery in Międzyrzecz Podlaski, sixty miles north of Lublin, looks impressive. At least from the outside. A high brick wall bounds a good-size piece of land. I open the heavy iron gate. Right inside, on the grounds of the cemetery, stands the caretaker's house. At the sight of me a powerful German shepherd almost breaks his chain. Summoned by the barking, a fat man appears from the depths of the house. We talk about the cemetery for a moment.

The caretaker has lived here since 1945.

The Germans left the cemetery in ruins. The gravestones were smashed to pieces, broken and shattered by bullets, since the Gestapo set up a shooting range here. The walls were also partly destroyed and partly torn down. The bricks had been required for other purposes.

Not long after the war a married couple named Finkilsztejn arrived from New York. They came from Międzyrzecz, and had decided to restore the cemetery. It was then that the murdered Jews were exhumed and buried in a common grave. The walls were rebuilt, scattered *matzevahs* were put back together, and those that lay in the right places were repaired. The caretaker leads me around the cemetery. In its depths, sheep are grazing.

"What I don't mow, they eat," he says, as if he wants to forestall my question.

The cemetery is old. Many of the *matzevahs* come from the eighteenth and nineteenth centuries. Some of them are cast iron, unique and beautifully ornamented monuments of funereal art. Międzyrzecz was a rich town. Before the war, Gentiles were a minority in a population of more than ten thousand. "Once upon a time the local count gave municipal and industrial privileges to the Jews and land to the Christians," the caretaker explains. There were beautiful synagogues here. One of them, from the eighteenth century and built of powerful stone blocks, was famous. It took the Germans more than a month to demolish it during the war.

The Jews of Międzyrzecz were famous as outstanding brushmakers and tanners. Their specialty, hard leather, was sold all over Poland and around the world. The secret of its manufacture was handed down from father to son. "This was 'little America'—that's what they used to say themselves," the caretaker concludes.

"How many Jews were saved and returned after the war?" I ask.

"How many were saved I don't know, but very few returned. Perhaps ten."

"Do they still live here?"

"No, there are no Jews here anymore. The last one died five years ago. He lies there"—the caretaker points into the shadows of the cemetery.

"I know, though, that one is left for sure. It's him I'm looking for."

The caretaker shakes his head decisively.

"He has a Polish wife and he changed his name," I add.

"Now that's another story. Anastazy Domański. Of course, I know him. He's a brushmaker. He lives on Polna Street, number 37. Only he's sort of Jew-non-Jew, you know?"

"I know."

The eighth member of the Lublin *minyan* has been baptized.

Klubowe

An hour later I am sitting with Domański in a meadow near the forest. It was impossible to remain at his home because his wife is ill and perhaps reluctant about conversations of this nature. So Domanski proposed a walk to the nearby oak grove. Here, among the tall grass, he spread his coat. "We'll be able to have a heart-to-heart talk," he said as he sat down and took out a pack of cheap cigarettes.

He is surprised when I tell him how I found him. "Didn't they give you my address in Lublin? They know it well enough."

"They gave it, but not the complete address," I throw in, not wanting to hurt him.

Still, Domański makes a dismissive gesture. "I know, they're a little ashamed of me, even though I often lead their prayers for them."

The old man lights a cigarette and unexpectedly bursts into tears.

"Something forced me to change my name, the way they killed those two ... a young couple in the very flower of life ... Sara was your age. She died in my arms ... I am Kagan, Natan Kagan."

The man pulls a handkerchief out of his pocket and wipes his eyes.

"When was that?" I ask.

"In forty-six. Didn't you see their graves in the cemetery?"

"Now I remember two stones near the entrance."

"They killed them, they killed them ..."

"How did it happen?"

"I wasn't there when it happened. People only called me afterward. Bandits broke into the house at night and shot them both."

"Were they caught?"

Preceding page:
Anastazjan Domański,
also known as Natan Kagan.

"Back there, then ..."

Kagan's head droops, and he wipes his eyes again. After a moment he speaks.

"I would never have decided to marry her, but she saved my life. She ran a private restaurant in those days, well known in town. I used to go there after work. I was a master brushmaker. She always pampered me. That evening she gave me an excellent meal. I ate until somebody came up and said, 'How about a half bottle, Master?' 'Why not,' I answered, and told her, 'Vodka here.' I was already half-soused, so when we drank more, I was finished. They carried me to the couch in the little room out behind the dining room. I woke up after maybe an hour and made for the door, but she wouldn't let me go. 'I ask you by all the saints, Natan, don't go.' I stayed, and if I hadn't listened I wouldn't have been alive after that night."

"What happened?"

"Around midnight one thug came to my home. He started banging on the window frame so loudly that the neighbor upstairs opened his window and shouted, 'What do you want?' He asked, 'Where is Kagan?' 'He might have gone to Lublin,' the neighbor answered. That only made him more angry. He pounded on the window until it broke. Then he went to a restaurant, but a different one. He was drunk, really drunk, and he went wild. He shot somebody. Somebody called Gruszka."

"A Jew?"

"No, a Pole. But he was looking for Jews and when he didn't find any, he had to take it out on somebody."

"And afterwards you stayed with that woman?"

"With Domańska. Yes. I took her name. I went to church. Had to ..."

"And was that the end of the threats?"

"The evil times passed. Besides, she was watching out for me."

"When did you start going to the synagogue again?"

"I traveled to Lublin for the first time six years ago. They received me badly. I'm not surprised. You know, I'm *mechuts.* I walked in and they said, 'You're Anastazjan Domański now and not Kagan. You talk Polish good, you talk beautifully, grammatically. You're not one of us anymore.' "

"Did they throw you out?"

"Throw me out or not, they acted as if I wasn't there. But afterward, when others died, then I joined them at prayers, too."

"They took you back."

"What could they do? They wouldn't have had a *minyan.*"

"What's it like now?"

"They're used to me."

"For thirty years you lived far from Jews, far from their religion."

"I didn't forget. During those years I forgot nothing. You can't forget that. It's not like this grass." Kagan leans forward and pulls out a handful of grass with a violent motion. He raises it and waves it in front of my eyes. "Not like grass, that I can pull up by the roots and that's that."

"I understand that you could not forget your Jewishness, but why did you return to it?"

"I didn't return for business, or for any kind of profit. I returned to my own faith so that my bones can rest beside those of my father."

The last two members of the *minyan* reside in Łuków, fifty-five miles from Lublin, on the same street, the town's main street. First, I find number 45. A small house. A middle-aged woman opens the door.

"Herszel Golman? He's not here anymore. He moved out."

"How's that? Where to?"

"He was old and his wife died. He felt worse and worse. About two months ago his son came and took him to Legnica."

"For good?"

"Yes. He gave us his place. A good man. We've known him for a long time. He said he might come to visit us sometime. Do you want to see him? I can give you his new address. He left it just in case."

"No, thank you. Legnica is at the other end of Poland. I have no reason to go there."

Number 78 is a good-size apartment house. On the second floor I knock on apartment 5. There is a visiting card in the door: "Pinkie and Lidia Fiksman." I knock for a long time. Silence. When I am ready to leave, thinking that there is no one there, I hear the shuffling of shoes behind the door and a woman's wary voice: "Who's there?"

I introduce myself. The woman begins questioning me. Where are you from? What do you want? Who sent you? I repeat all my references to the closed door, but it has no effect. I go on explaining. The woman seems to hesitate. At last she asks, "What is my first name?" Without pause I answer, saying a name different than the one that is printed on the card. "Leiba. Leiba Fiksman."

That does the trick. The door slowly opens. Behind it stands a small, corpulent woman with an expressive face. "Well, come in, then," she says with a cautious smile.

The apartment is small. The kitchen contains a tile stove, and the room is divided in half by a tattered brown screen. On one side stands a chest and a round table, and on the other side a wardrobe and a bed covered with a down comforter. The woman apologizes for her behavior, but since the death of her husband, she has been afraid of attacks. These are such uncertain times, and there is nobody to protect an old woman.

"Your husband is dead?" I ask, shocked.

"He died. He died, the poor man," Leiba Fiksman says. "He was ninety-two and his time had come. I am left alone. The last Jew in town."

She falls silent and then adds, after a moment: "I am left alone not only in this town, but alone in the world. They are all gone, all dead."

I start to say that I'm sorry, that I sympathize, but I stop myself because each word seems too shallow and dry. Neither of us speaks for a long moment, and then Leiba suddenly becomes animated.

"You can help me. You travel around the country and know so many Jews. Please find me somebody, a companion, I ask you."

"But who?"

"Some person—a Jewish woman. She can even be fifty, she can even have a daughter. I will feed her and clothe her. That will be a lucky woman. I don't have a lot of money, but I have wealth. I have my husband's fur coat, my fur, a lot of clothes, a tea service and a table setting for twelve ... When I die, she will inherit it all. The apartment, too. Now it's so difficult with apartments, you have to wait so many years. It's a perfect chance, right?"

The woman looks at me anxiously. I know that I cannot say no. Leiba is more and more excited.

"I have a feeling that you are going to help me. You are a good person. God might have sent you to me. Because I am very religious. In the past perhaps less, even though I came from a devout family and I graduated from *cheder* and the Hebrew high school. But I loved to read secular books more than anything. I read so much that I ruined my eyes. But now I read only the *sidur*, the Jewish prayer book. Especially on Fridays. And on Saturday I lie in bed all day and I hardly get up and I pray and pray. Because you know, I have sinned a great deal."

Leiba stops speaking. She is obviously wavering: What to say next? After a moment she goes on in a hushed voice. "I have been angry at our Lord."

"How?" I ask, surprised.

The old woman nods her head. "Oh, yes. Yes. Because we are supposed to be a chosen people and—what? Blood and blood and hatred. Sometimes I thought about it and ... and I still think that way a little—it would have been better if He had not chosen us, if He had let us live like others."

Leiba Fiksman at her home.

CHAPTER TWO

THE LONG WAY HOME

There is a group of young Jews in Warsaw, and they are praying and keeping the Sabbath and learning Yiddish and even organizing lectures. Such news began circulating around the city in early 1981. This was the time of Solidarity's blossoming, a time of great political tension but also of an explosion of long-stifled social needs. People could finally do what they wanted. And even though many restrictions remained, the range of freedom was enormous in comparison to the previous thirty-five years.

Dozens of independent organizations and associations sprang up; conferences and symposia were held on previously forbidden topics; hundreds of new magazines, bulletins, and newspapers—often uncensored—were published; and monuments were hurriedly erected to national heroes who had previously been passed over in silence. But even against this tumultuous background, the information about young, religious, "conscious" Jews evoked astonishment. Older Jews were the most incredulous. Their children had, for the most part, emigrated, and those who had stayed in Poland were completely assimilated. And there are still "that kind" here? Impossible!

Nevertheless, there were. Staszek Krajewski, his wife Monika, Kostek Gebert, Rysia Zachariasz, Basia Kawalec, and others had found their identity. We met them in the spring of 1981. Afterward I accompanied these people, my contemporaries, through the next four years of trying to understand and describe their complicated fates.

Staszek Krajewski during the kiddush prayers that begin the Sabbath observances.

"Who is a Jew?"

Staszek Krajewski smiles.

"Well, that's a very hard question."

"And, after the experiences of the last few decades, an unpopular one. But let's talk about it. In the past, when Jews constituted a caste, they were distinguished—strongly—by language, religion, customs, dress. How is it today?"

"To me the distinguishing factor is religion. Among Jews this is connected in a subtle but very important way with nationality. It was exactly through religion that the Jews became the Chosen People. When someone coverted to Judaism—it has been this way since ancient times—they were accepted into the religion and into the nation. In Israel, despite numerous efforts, they have been unable to think up any other criterion and this one is still applied."

"And yet there exist unbelieving Jews."

"A lot of them. From the beginning of the century a certain percentage of Jews has been laicizing, although it usually happens that a complete break with religion ends in degeneration. But of course there are many other viewpoints on this matter."

"Such as?"

"Most acknowledge as Jews only those who live as Jews. By this they mean, aside from religion, the whole Jewish tradition and culture. The widest definition of a Jew encompasses all those who are thought of as Jews."

"And in Poland?"

"Usually the second criterion is applied, although it happens—and this strikes me as completely acceptable—that a Jew is simply someone who feels like one. But then again, self-definition is subjective by nature and as such it can change."

"Like with you?"

"Exactly. Until I was a teenager I knew absolutely nothing about my Jewish background. I didn't connect it with my family at all. I remember that when we had to write an essay in school on the twentieth anniversary of the uprising in the Warsaw ghetto, I copied mine out of some book and I didn't have the slightest feeling that it had anything to do with me."

"When did you find out?"

"In 1964 I went to Israel to visit my grandfather, my mother's father. But the strange thing was that this didn't really change my outlook either. I still didn't regard myself as at all connected with Jews, with Israel. To such a degree that when they asked me if I wanted to stay there, I didn't understand the question. After all, you have relatives in various countries—a grandfather in Israel, an uncle in Argentina, but we are all Poles."

"Afterward, though, it all stopped being so straightforward."

"The turning point was March of sixty-eight. That made me aware that I am of Jewish origin, that it counts, and that I can be beaten up for it."

"Were you beaten?"

"Not literally, but I took the anti-Semitic propoganda very

personally. I found myself in a position where some people were telling me, 'Get out of here, Jew!' I could disagree and put up arguments but that doesn't change anything because such people aren't going to be convinced. Our generation and those younger are an exception. They have never seen a Jew—except for a completely assimilated one—with their own eyes and they have only absorbed outside opinions without thinking. But you can talk to them. As I see it, for them, the fact that a Jew turns out to be somebody they know can have a positive meaning. Anyway, from 1968 on I've had to face that problem—like, every Jew in Poland. It's constantly with me."

"Are you still helpless against that 'get out'?"

"In a sense, yes. Of course, I don't think that those people have a right to talk that way, but they are deeply convinced. My reaction can be either to laugh it off or to appeal to others who counter it and say 'nonsense'."

"Isn't the fact that you regard it as nonsense enough?"

"Somehow no. . . . Of course, there is one effective method. To say, 'All right, I'll get out,' and leave. Then there is no problem."

"You didn't leave."

"Among Jews there is an idea that you have to act appropriately, which means to turn around, walk out, and slam the door, but after all it isn't over when you slam the door. To leave the country and your friends and often your family and start over somewhere. And me? Hard to say. It just happened. I deeply disagreed with what was going on. I didn't want to leave. So, well, I stayed."

"How old were you?"

"Eighteen."

"Did March, sixty-eight, change you?"

"No. March was important, it was a watershed, but afterwards what had been awakened fell dormant."

"I well remember the shock that March represented to me and Jewish friends of mine. It's hard to believe that it could fall dormant. Maybe you wanted it to turn out that way. Maybe you *wanted* to stay unaware."

"Yes, you're right. I suppressed it forcibly. Jewishness had been thrust upon me, and I felt a need to push free of it. At a certain moment I even disliked Jews. Well, I wasn't an anti-Semite..."

"Before the war there were a couple of belligerant anti-Semites of Jewish origin."

"That's perfectly explicable in psychological terms. I experienced my Jewishness as a hunchback feels his hump. Thus there was something in myself that I strongly disliked. After all, it is possible not to accept oneself, even to hate oneself, and also to hate those who remind me by their very existence that I am a Jew.

"I went through convulsive changes. I was happy to discover that those excellent people that I admired were Jews, and so many of them were Nobel Prize winners. I remember how incredibly eagerly I leafed through the bibliographies of serious works of philosophy and how I latched with great satisfaction onto the large number of Jewish names. Or, again, how I was walking along Krupówki shortly after March with a friend and a bully coming in the other direction said, 'You, kike!' We argued about who he said it to and each of us insisted that he was the one. So there was shame, and also pride. Except that there was more shame."

"What do you think are the sources of that shame?"

"Back then I knew nothing about Jews, their culture and religion and language, so Jewishness had no positive associations for me. I think that situation is characteristic of the majority of people of Jewish extraction in Poland. They know neither the Jewish past nor the tradition, so their origins are only a mark of shame."

"Doesn't that result in large measure from the fact that Jews in postwar Poland come predominantly from communist families and are either communists themselves or former communists who have consciously turned away from that tradition?"

"Yes, that's very important. My family is such an example. My father's father broke all links with his home by becoming a communist. So my father did not know his paternal grandparents, did not even know who they were."

"And on the side of your father's mother, your grandmother, it's even stronger. You are descended in a direct line from Adolf Warski, one of the most famous communist activists in the history of Poland. The shipyard in Szczecin, the second largest shipyard in the country after the Lenin yard in Gdańsk, is named after him."

"Yes, Adolf Warski was my great-grandfather. From the beginning of the thirties, my father lived together with Grandfather Warski and his family in Moscow. They all died there during the Stalinist purges.

Only my father, who was a young boy then, survived."

"Didn't he turn away from communism?"

"No. He thought those were terrible things, but he still went on believing. Communism was an expanding ideology then. For many the war was proof that the old bourgeois order had failed and a new order had to be built."

"And your mother?"

"It was a little different with Mom. She came from an average family, and when she turned communist, she was the first to break with tradition. She was taken deep into the Soviet Union with her father and brother, and there she survived the war. Later my grandfather and uncle emigrated, but Mom chose Poland and the system. My parents had no other tradition to offer me besides communism, and when they revised their views—you know, the famous revisionism—even that ideology was gone. So I was left empty-handed."

"And you had to do it yourself."

"I looked around blindly. The beginning was typical for our generation: being a hippie, Eastern religion."

"Zen Buddhism?"

"Sure. You know those fads. But there had to be something deeper. Afterward, when I stopped being a hippie, I began to be seriously interested in Christianity. I read a lot, I went to church sometimes, and at a certain moment I wanted to become a Catholic. I tried shyly to convince a certain priest to convert me. I wanted someone to convince me. We talked, but nothing came of it."

"Maybe you chose the wrong priest."

"The priest was outstanding. It was I who couldn't believe that Jesus of Nazareth was God. The man might have been a great teacher, a master, but for someone who started out as an atheist it is very difficult to believe that he is God. I know that there are converts among Jews, but that was as far as I could go. That was the crucial point for me. I had to turn back. And so in the end I arrived at Judaism."

"Wait a minute—that's a little too smooth."

"Well, that is not right, because it was hard. I had been brought up not only without religion, but in real opposition to it."

"What, specifically, did that mean?"

"The conviction that religion was for stupid and ignorant people. That it is a relic, something like the subjective experience of art, except that art is better because it develops. For a long time that was what I believed."

"So where did your interest in religion come from?"

"You could say that at first I followed in my parents' footsteps. They, as communists, believed in the possibility of transforming society, in the malleability of human nature, almost like a religion. It was a faith but young, less revered, and as it turned out, weak. Thence the desire to know those other faiths—powerful, with primeval mystical sources. That is important as background. Next came pondering á lâ Dostoyevsky: Why should we do good? And here I was astounded to discover that through attaching such great importance to morality, my home had been religious in a certain sense. There had been no creed or liturgy, but the moral tension that it left me with surely played a large role in what I was going through.

"You were seeking God. Does that mean that you believed in His existence?"

"I had read, for instance, about the existence of the God of the philosophers, and I accepted that, but further on it said that there is also the God of Abraham, Jacob and Isaac. That struck me as strange. And I remember an important moment later. A Frenchwoman whom I knew wrote me a letter, á lâ Sartre: Man is alone, understanding is impossible, and so on. It all seemed accurate—I had experienced similar things myself, but as soon as I started walking through the city to set down my answer, it came to me that after all there is understanding among people because God stands behind them. That was the crucial moment. Quite recently I learned that Rosenzweig and Buber had similar experiences. And furthermore that Buber, before he took of Chassidism, had immersed himself in Buddhism. And if we're talking about me, it was also important, as I realized only years later, that I had always had a religious nature. That gave me a stubborn sense of purpose. In spite of failures, I went on looking for so long that I managed to find my answer."

"Does that mean that you no longer have doubts?"

"Of course there are many things about Judaism that I have doubts about; yet I fit there. It is a field where I can look for a place to dig a hole and plant my little roots. And if you ask me whether I believe..."

"I am asking."

"I would answer: at times. But I have faith that the sources are alive. And I am not only talking about religion, but also about entering into a certain tradition."

"Until then you hadn't known the tradition and, what's more, you had rejected it in advance along with everything connected with Jewishness."

"Overcoming that lasted years and, as I can see today, had two sides. This is not only my experience, but also that of some of my friends. First there are things that lend themselves to psychotherapy—complexes, behavior in the face of anti-Semitism, saying out loud: 'I am a Jew.' Because you have to accept your Jewishness in order to be able to do something good with it. Kostek and the others had exactly that kind of psychoanalytic group, and I was lucky because many years earlier I had met Monika. She was the first person in my life—it was incredible to me—who could pronounce the word 'Jew' in a completely normal tone of voice. And furthermore, even though she was not a Jew, she took an active interest in Jewish culture. With Monika, I could at last talk about everything I had always wanted to, but had never managed to discuss even with my closest friends. Of course, to avoid further oversimplifications, that process—let's call it psychotherapeutic—was slow and complicated."

"How long have you and Monika been married?"

"Eleven years. In 1984, during our stay in the U.S., Monika converted to Judaism."

"And what constituted the second part of these changes?"

"Knowledge. Eight years ago Monika and I were in the synagogue during *Pesach* for the first time, and afterward at the *seder* at the Jewish *Kehilla* in Warsaw. It made a horrible impression on us. The building was fit for demolition, the cafeteria was unspeakable, the cooks slobbering, and across from me sat an old man spilling his broth all over the table and his prayer book. Somebody, presumably a rabbi, was praying and bobbing when children suddenly appeared in the doorway. 'Sara, *kum hier*!' he shouted, and went on singing. We almost got up and left and we didn't go back for years. We knew nothing then; we didn't know the ritual or what it was about and we could see only the external form, which was more or less repugnant."

"Now you know."

"I know a lot more, but still little. It's terribly difficult to find anything on the subject. I searched, I read, I talked, and I also went with Monika to the old Jewish cemeteries she was photographing."

"And you came back to the synagogue."

"To the degree that we go for the major holidays and I have even got used to that style and come to like it. But it's still not wholly my place, because the atmosphere that prevails among those old people is—how should I put it?—terminal, as if something is coming to an end, and I am at exactly the other stage."

"Every Friday you observe the *Shabbat* at home."

"Ritual opens up a certain sphere that otherwise cannot be discovered. That is why it is indispensable. I understood that long ago, but in the first place, I was a complete ignoramus and in the second, ritual requires a certain social dimension, even a mini-society, and so only when we had gathered a group of people who were in a similar situation did we try. A more experienced friend led the *seder* at our home. That started several of us going further in that direction. Kostek started *Shabbats*, and soon we did, too."

"Who showed you the observances?"

"Nobody. We taught ourselves from American books."

"Judaism was, and in its Orthodox variant is, an integral religious system that introduces the sacred into every area of life, an order of laws based on harsh and comprehensive rules of behavior. What is Judaism for you?"

"My ideal is the most authentic Orthodox Judaism. It simultaneously attracts and repels me. Then again, Reform Judaism is more realistic. In practice it means enriching the life that we lead here and now with certain elements that give it a new dimension. I choose what is possible and what strikes me as attractive. This principle is somewhat suspect—on what basis do I choose? That is why confidence and faith are needed at the outset. So far, I have not failed. The *Shabbat*, for instance, provides a certain rhythm: light the candles every week, bless the food, sing something, read from the Bible. That's the way it looks."

"In its external dimension."

"The *Shabbat* is supposed to be a foretaste of eternal life. You have to break away completely. This is difficult, and the consciousness that it should be that way is another obstacle. But I get a great deal out of it. Remember, I spoke about my religious inclination, but it had been suspended—I never felt like a participant, much less like a creator. Now I have found both those elements."

"Doesn't it seem to you sometimes that this is just something you have made up, read about?"

"Sometimes I ask myself if it all makes sense. But only sometimes, because after all, I have experienced something and I am still experiencing it, and God speaks to each person in His own language."

Kostek Gebert has traveled a similar road. He is, along with Staszek, the strongest personality in this group of young Jews who have discovered their identity. For all of them, now in their thirties, the turning point was March, 1968. Like their Polish contemporaries who were then studying in the universities of Warsaw, Krakow, or Gdansk, they call themselves the March '68 Generation. Back then the police brutally routed demonstrations for the democratization of university life. It was a shock for young people. To young Jews it was a double shock. The student riots ended up becoming a pretext for a mass purge of the Party and the power structure by the ruling circles. This was done to the tune of anti-Semitic slogans. As a result of the action, tens of thousands of Jews left Poland. Those who stayed were changed people.

This is what happened to Kostek, who, even though he was still in high school, was as strongly affected by the March events as were the university students. Until that moment everything had been so clear for him. Raised in a communist family by parents who held high positions in the *aparat*, he believed that Poland was the best place in the world and that the regime prevailing there was the only proper system. Kostek regarded himself as a Pole, and the fact that his mother was of Jewish extraction caused him no problems. Now his black-and-white world lay in ruins, and he stood defenseless and alone before his own Jewishness, which had assumed significance in a sudden and brutal way.

The shame was a piercing feeling. A Jew was something unimportant; worse, something trivial. He tried to comfort himself with the thought of Einstein, Freud, and the Bible, but the stereotypical Jewish bumpkin who messed his pants from fear at the slightest provocation always crawled to the surface. Later, to save himself, Kostek plunged to the other extreme. He exalted himself. He saw that Jews were the Chosen Ones, suffering for others and better than anyone else. But this ideal of the Jew did not fit any person he knew, or himself. The difference between imagination and reality caused a growing depression. It lasted for months, and then, in December, 1970, the massacre of workers in Gdansk and Szczecin occurred. The police fired on striking shipyard workers. Many were killed. It was all too much, and the neurotic seventeen-year-old decided to take his own life. A sentimental gesture saved him. After swallowing a large quantity of sleeping powder, he decided to say farewell to his parents. They thought something was amiss. They took him to the hospital in time.

Afterward, it was very bad. His frightened mother took Kostek from psychologist to psychiatrist. No results. Finally they hit on a famous professor. As always, Kostek mumbled something about himself. In reply the professor told how, in the bloodiest days of Stalin's terror, a KGB agent had come for his father in Moscow. His father said good-bye with the words, "Remember to go to school tomorrow." He never saw his father again. "That cured me," Kostek recalls.

The next years were a period of seeking, but free of the previous hysterical floundering. Without flaunting his differentness, Kostek changed direction. He became a psychologist. He discovered the Polish tradition, freedom-loving and aristocratic, that had been as absent from his home as the Jewish tradition. Atheism was no longer enough for him. Along with a whole generation, he was fascinated by the religions of the Far East. He discovered Judaism by accident. During a stay in the United States, he met a cousin. It was amazing—his cousin was simply a Jew, without complexes and without crowing about it. Together they spent the first *Shabbat* of Kostek's life. "That was a great experience," he says. "I immediately felt at home."

After returning to Poland he began to be more deeply interested in Jewish religion and culture. Then came the turning point. Outside Warsaw there was a workshop for psychotherapists. He found himself among many people of Jewish extraction there. During group therapy the problem of "being a Jew" came up with unusual sharpness. For most of them it was the first chance in their lives to say out loud, "I am a Jew." There was also astonishment and joy at finding others who had similar problems, fears, and wounds. Kostek defines it concisely: "I burst."

The workshop ended, but they remained a group. Loose at first. They met to talk, and it quickly became evident that they knew nothing. They did not know the history of the Jews or their traditions and culture.

So they decided to learn together. Thus the Jewish Flying University (JFU) was born.

It was a completely private activity. They met in apartments to hear reports or met with known Jewish activists, writers, and actors. The lectures covered many topics: the Sephardim, the Frankists, the Chassidim, the problem of assimilation, the Thirteen Articles of Faith, the Chosen People of the Bible, Jewish holidays, kibbutzim, the Central Committee of Jews in Poland, Freud, Kafka and Jewish mysticism, the symbolism of wine and light in the *Shabbat*, the Łódź ghetto... Some of the subjects they researched themselves, and for others they invited people with professional knowledge. Often these were Jews from America, England, or Israel who were passing through Warsaw.

More than a dozen and sometimes several scores of people came to the meetings. There was, however, a constant group: Staszek Krajewski, his wife Monika, Kostek, Rysia Zachariasz, Basia Kawalec. They were the ones who found the lecturers, informed the participants, and spoke up most often in discussion.

The JFU came to an end the moment martial law was introduced in December, 1981. Its legend persisted, however, along with the friendships that had been formed. Kostek does not regret its ending. He thinks that the JFU had its best days behind it. And while it had satisfied the needs of some, it had awakened the needs of others, who can now consciously go on developing.

That is what Kostek is doing. In 1980 he began his first serious attempts at religion. At first everything was exceedingly difficult. There was no one to show him how to keep the *Shabbat* or celebrate *Pesach*, nobody to initiate him into rituals and customs that seemed, from the outside, foreign and incomprehensible. So he taught himself from American books. "That was murder," he recalls. "I was too busy watching the sequence of prayers to feel anything."

Years would have to pass before the form became routine and stopped dominating over the content, before Kostek and his family found a shared value in it. Every Friday his wife Małgosia bakes a splendid *challah* and says a blessing. Their two children, too small to take part in the late *Shabbat* supper, already understand well that it is a special evening.

"And you?" I ask Kostek. "Who are you now after all these experiences?"

"I am a Polish Jew. That is not only a term but an identity. In many, many respects I can talk better with Poles than with Jews from the States or Israel, even though I feel an emotional affinity with them. I feel best with Polish Jews. Except that there aren't any."

"Don't you feel, then, that what you are doing in this small group is a kind of museum exhibit? An artificial holding on..."

"Certainly it was artificial when we started. I even called it archaeology. But now it has become genuine. I began with the *Shabbat* and it is no longer a reconstruction. It is my own. Without it I would be poorer and more lonely."

"But that is only the beginning."

"Yes, but I am not in a hurry. Religion has enormous significance for me. I also know that I will not become an Orthodox Jew, so whichever injunctions I observe, I observe with the greatest understanding and scrupulousness. And that takes time. I began with ritual because that is the most difficult threshold to cross. The second element is learning, studying Scripture. But working with texts comes naturally to me. I only have one problem—I don't know Hebrew and I have to read everything in translation. Many cabbalistic and chassidic texts have made a big impression on me, even though I know that in translation they are poorer by half, and who knows if that isn't the more important half? Still, they retain reflections of that richness. For instance, in Rabbi Nachman of Braclaw, who was an atypical pessimistic Chassid, perhaps even existential, I found ideas that were developed much later by humanistic psychology."

"Do you read according to any plan?"

"No, and that's my problem. I am always uneasy; I feel like a savage who has been let into a library and has learned to read a little. He grabs a book here, a book there, pieces something together, but he remains a savage. A normal Jew begins in *cheder* and learns the methodological and theological basics so that he knows how to make use of that library that has grown over five thousand years. I lack that. Nor do I have a master to guide me."

"You won't find one here."

"And so I have a dream of going for a year to the U.S., to some rabbi."

"And yet in Poland you give lectures in various places, you tell people about the history of the Jews, about the Cabbals, about Chassidism. You are an authority."

NAUKA HISTORII W UPADKU
PRASA POLSKA
HISTORIA KOLORU
wprowadzenie do psychologii
To Pray as a Jew

Uprising in the Warsaw Ghetto
A Little Boy in Search of God
in der deutschen Geschichte
BOŻNICE DREWNIANE
BUBER
Alexandre Safran
la cabale
Payot

A seder in the apartment of Monika and Staszek Krajewski.

*Preceding page:
Kostek Gebert, with his daughter in his apartment.*

"When they ask me to talk about something, I have a feeling both of my own drastic incompetence and, at the same time, with so few of us here, of drastic competence. And besides, I accept these offers because I like doing it."

"But isn't it a dangerous situation in a psychological sense? Dangerous like everything done without social supervision, without, if I may say so, competition?"

"Of course it is. I even went through a period of 'Jewish chic.' It passed. I understand that you don't have to be a mouthy Jew. That is immodest."

"So what should you be?"

"When he was dying, Reb Zusja said, 'In that world they won't ask me why I wasn't Moses. They will only ask me why I wasn't Zusja.' That's the way it is with me. I have no ambition to be Moses. I want to be Kostek."

"What does that mean in practice?"

"Choice. And as I see it, cultivating my Jewishness is also important, so that I can be a decent husband and father and so that Poland can someday be the way we want it to be. That is why, even if learning Hebrew and studying the *Talmud* are important, I have no ultimate conviction that I should devote so much time to them at the expense of other things. I now think that I don't have to be—and even shouldn't be—the wisest Jew; that it will be much better if I am a good Jew. And that, too, is difficult."

"Why?"

"It takes a certain humility. A long time went by before I admitted that Staszek had read more than I, had thought things over, and that he was more conscientious and ought to be a certain authority to me. That was not easy."

"How do you see the future?"

"I believe that we are the last ones. Definitely."

"How can you live with such an awareness?"

"It's difficult."

"And there will be no Jews in Poland?"

"In the sense of a religious, national group, no. Poland will once again have had a piece of its past and its culture amputated."

"Why has that happened?"

"There was an enormous string of coincidences. First it caused the flowering of Jewish culture on Polish soil and then, in changed circumstances, its destruction."

"That destruction was Hitler's doing, but people also say that Polish anti-Semitism played a part in the complete disappearance of that community."

"There is some truth in that. With this fundamental reservation: that I distinguish what happened before the war, when anti-Semitism was moderate in the sense that it did not have murderous intentions, from the immediate postwar period when it did."

"And the war?"

"I would put the period of the war in parentheses here because it was a totally extreme situation and Poles were next in line for the gas."

"How is it today?"

"Anti-Semitism shackles the Polish consciousness. Not murderous, of course, but judgmental, moderate. On the other hand, though on a smaller scale, an irrational philo-Semitism is also appearing."

"Where do these attitudes come from, when there are no Jews?"

"Exactly from the fact that there are none. As a result, attitudes toward them result not from real experience, but from mythologized positive or negative imaginings. In the case of anti-Semitism, parental structures and, often, political manipulation come into play.

"Let me tell you a story. In the late seventies I was returning from the mountains by train with a fine intelligent boy. We talked half the night, and at the end he said, 'You know Hitler did one thing for us—he solved the Jewish problem.' I replied, 'Hey fellow, I'm a Jew.' And he said, 'So tell me, do you slaughter children for matzo?' He was no anti-Semite. He simply wanted to know. He explained to me that there are various barbarous customs. The Aztecs tore out hearts..."

"And isn't anything changing here?"

"Little. Textbooks, guides, museums say nothing about the annihilation; they cover up the murderous postwar anti-Semitism and the moderate prewar anti-Semitism. What is worse, 'unofficial' Poland is not speaking up on this matter. With few exceptions."

"I can see that it pains you greatly, because your expression has changed."

"A great deal. I've had it up to here with explaining to my Polish friends that everything is not in order on the Jewish question, and to my

Jewish friends that Poles are not a nation of cannibals. And every time I have to throw my authority into the scales."

"Once, telling me about the workshop, you said that one of the most important discoveries was that Jews are linked by one thing—fear."

"That's right, a great deep fear ready to explode at any instant. And that is the only thing that truly distinguishes my experience of Jews and non-Jews. The former feel it the same way I do; the latter, at the best of times, can understand it."

"And how is it now? Does that fear still accompany you?"

"At this moment it is tamed. Long ago I suppressed it; I didn't want to see it in general, so it exploded and disorganized my life. Later, thanks most of all to the Jewish Flying University, that fear stopped being a shameful conundrum and it no longer rules me."

"But you feel it?"

"Uncommonly seldom."

"When?"

"Sometimes purely accidentally, irrationally. And sometimes it results from some anti-Semitic behavior. Once, for instance, I dressed like a Jew, in a long white shirt, a *yarmulka* on my head, and went out into the street. I got onto a streetcar and at once I felt that people were staring at me strangely. They began making comments. Not so much aggressively as in astonishment, with a shade of contempt. 'Look—they didn't gas them all...' Someone immediately said, 'You can't talk that way because he hears everything.' And an old man said, 'What do you mean? He's from America. There are no young Jews in Poland anymore.'"

"Why don't you leave?"

"I've already told you. I'm a Polish Jew. And besides, there's something that I would call the obligation of faithfulness. I think that's the best way of summing up what we're doing, Staszek, Monika, Rysia, me."

"Explain this to me more specifically."

"Behind me stands the long, long history of my family and my nation. The most important thing was always for the children to grow up as Jews. If, knowing what I know today, I turned away from that, it would be a contradiction of everything they did through the centuries. It would mean that they should have assimilated long ago and that the Holocaust was a punishment for stupidity. The murder of millions would have no other value beyond the biological threat."

"I understand that this is a certain moral imperative."

"I could formulate that imperative like this: so that my children can be Jews. So that they can have a chance."

"That is personal. What about social? After all, it is public knowledge that if someone has 'Jewish problems' he can turn to you or Staszek. Many young Jews gather around you."

"It seems to me that what we are doing for Jews here has a certain value. Because if they turn away from Jewishness, they do it with a consciousness of what they are leaving behind, and if they return, they know better than we did what they are returning to. And even though I know it will sound overstated, I want to say one more thing. In this improbable slaughter that was carried out here, a chance was left to me to live. From that comes an obligation which, after long suffering, I accept with joy."

April 19, 1985. The forty-second anniversary of the Warsaw Ghetto Uprising. The official ceremony took place in the morning. Now, in the afternoon, the square in front of the Heroes of the Ghetto Monument is empty. On the benches mothers sit in the sun with their small children, and old men read newspapers. Off to one side stands a small group of people. Thirty, perhaps forty persons. Mostly young, some of them holding children by the hand. The men have *yarmulkas* on their heads. They are gathered close together, conversing in hushed voices.

After a long moment they form a column. They move towards the monument. Staszek and Kostek walk at the front. They are carrying a large, beautiful wreath. The inscription on the ribbon, in Hebrew and Polish, reads, "We Are Your Children."

Staszek Krajewski and Kostek Gebert at the Heroes of the Ghetto Monument.

CHAPTER THREE

I COULD HAVE BEEN A BILLIONAIRE

Zygmunt-Srul Warszawer
during prayers in the Warsaw synagogue.

The last kosher butcher in Warsaw is named Zygmunt Warszawer. As for a *shochet*, there is not a single one left in Poland. Both are needed for slaughtering. The first prepares the animal, helps kill it, and cuts the meat afterward. With one stroke of a thin knife, the second slices the throat of the cow and then inspects the carcass to make sure that it is not *trayf*. When the last *shochet* left for Israel, the Jewish community invited another from America. He returned home after a year. Now a *shochet* comes from Budapest once a month. He and Warszawer carry out the slaughtering in the municipal abattoir.

The shop where Warszawer sells kosher meat stands in the center of Praga.* There was no number to match the address I had been given. This did not worry me, since a shop is always easy to find. Nevertheless, I walked the whole street without result. No shop. I circled back, asking passersby. Of course, they knew various meat shops, but one like that? Some did not understand the word *kosher* at all. When I explained, they stared at me curiously. An old man asked, "Are you interested in Jews?" "Yes." "I'm a Jew." "Really?" "No, I'm kidding," he said and hurried away. Finally a hairdresser in a small beauty parlor pointed me toward a red building and a door in the courtyard.

The red building is in bad shape. There is no inscription, no sign, only the iron door hanging open. Later I learn that the open door is a signal to customers. It means that the shop is open—even in the coldest weather. The premises are large, high, and dark, with chipped and cracked tiles almost all the way up the walls. Blocked-off pipes stick out of the walls. Before the war this was a *mikva*, a ritual bath belonging to

*Praga—Large district of Warsaw on the right bank of the Vistula, across the river from the city center.

Warszawer's kosher butcher shop.

the prayer house next door, where children are playing on a vacant lot now. The Germans burned down the prayer house in 1943.

Even though it is very cold in the shop, the customers do not leave after making their purchases. They stand around the counter or sit on an old wooden bench. They are talking and joking loudly. In Polish, in Yiddish. Zygmunt, formerly Srul Warszawer, has been running the shop for twenty-eight years. At the beginning one of the directors told him that he was to sell only to Jews, but Warszawer retorted angrily, "I'm not going to start a ghetto! To me, everybody is equal." And so it has remained. Jews come because this is one of the few places in the city where they feel at home. Poles come because the meat is exceptionally good and also because they like Zygmunt.

A short, square-shouldered man of nearly seventy, Warszawer is in constant motion. He circulates among the clients, joking, pinching girls, carrying on conversations in muted tones with old men off to the side. Even the local drunks and thieves respect him. When he moved into the apartment next door to the shop more than a quarter-century ago, they immediately began loitering. One of them came into the shop once and flashed a switchblade. Warszawer told him that a gypsy does not steal where he lives. And he added, "I may be a Jew, but I am not afraid. You've got a knife, but I've got an ax." This was effective; Warszawer has always known how to get along with people. "That's why I'm alive," he says.

Half a year later, on a sweltering June evening, I am sitting with Zygmunt-Srul at the end of a long table. There are four tables. The table of honor stands on a small platform, and above it twinkle lights in the shape of a horseshoe, the symbol of luck, with a Virgin Mary in the middle. The other three tables, each more than thirty feet long, are set perpendicular to the table of honor. They are all covered with white tablecloths, and they are copiously laden. Dishes of homemade sausage sliced in thick chunks, roast chicken, herring, mountains of pickles nearby, and bowls full of wild mushrooms. And bottles—the bottles of vodka and the bottles of mineral water are being drained with equal expedition.

The guests are packed in tightly. Nearly three hundred people have come here for at least two days and two nights of raising the roof. Music spills through the flung-open doors. The orchestra is playing outside. Several couples have begun to dance on the wide planks, still smelling of sap, that have been laid on the bare earth. Nearby a hen that has managed to sneak out of the chicken coop is pecking in search of grain on the threshing floor.

A village wedding. The reception is being held in the barn. It has been painstakingly decorated. Carpets, images, and drawings hang on the wall beside the glimmering horseshoe and the ceiling has been completely concealed by strips of paper. Colorful, shiny, they sway softly above the heads of the increasingly merry, increasingly noisy guests. Right here, in this barn, Srul Warszawer had one of his hiding places forty years ago.

It was a den scooped out of the hay. He lay motionless in it for hours, alert and tense. He was hiding not only from the Germans, but also from the children of his hosts. The necessity of this had become obvious to him when he went to visit Franek Błachnio in nearby Leokadia; Franek's ten-year-old daughter told her mother, "Srul is here," and after that he was not allowed in the house. Franek would set bread, milk, and beets outside in the evenings, and Srul would take the food to the woods at night.

He was in hiding for twenty-six months. This hiding was a ceaseless moving from place to place—from woods to field to house to

barn, and two days later, somewhere else. He circulated that way among umpteen villages in the triangle formed by Łaskarzew, Sobolew, and Wilga, visiting every farm because he figured that if everyone helped him no one would turn him in—to do so would mean self-destruction. Today he includes all the guests in a sweeping wave of his hand and says, "My saviors."

They are here along with their children and their grandchildren. Zygmunt-Srul knows them all, and they know him. He is "Uncle" to hundreds of children. Even during weddings he slips them candy, of which he always has a full pocket. Every so often someone approaches and sits down. "Zygmunt, have a drink." "How are you feeling these days, Mr. Warszawer?" And later, when the outbursts of laughter almost drown the music, often: "This little Jew of ours is pretty neat, right?"

In 1939 there were several thousand Jews in the area. Perhaps ten survived the war. None stayed. Only Zygmunt-Srul still comes around, by train or bus now, visiting old acquaintances, attending every wedding, christening and funeral.

Warszawer, the guest of honor at the wedding, is shown with the bride and bridegroom.

He was born in Łaskarzew. Like all the little towns in the region, it was half Polish and half Jewish. Srul's father, devout and serious, owned a two-story building on the market square, a slaughterhouse, and a shop. He did business with the squires, the peasants, and at village fairs. He was president of the Jewish community and also, elected by Jews and Christians, a member of the town council. These functions absorbed his time and pulled him away from his business. So Srul, his sixth child took over.

Srul began riding to the villages and getting to know the peasants at a very young age. "I was their favorite," he recalls. "My word was sacred and they knew it. I never cheated anybody and I gave honest prices." He also lent money without interest, and when they could not repay him, which happened often because people in these parts were poor, he extended the debts, sometimes indefinitely. Thus, when the horrible times came, the peasants helped him. And not only the peasants.

It started at the beginning of the war. The first one to save Srul's life was Smarzewski, the prewar chief of police. Two trucks full of German police came to town. They took twenty-eight Jews. Warszawer was among them. Smarzewski walked up to the truck and asked, "Are you taking Poles, too?" That was a big risk, something they could have arrested him for. "No," snapped one of the police. "So," Smarzewski said sharply to Srul, "what are you doing here?" And he pushed him out of the lineup. The twenty-seven were shot in the nearby woods.

Smarzewski also took Srul in when he escaped with his four-year-old son from the camp in Wilga. After the liquidation of the Łaskarzew Jews, who were taken away in an unknown direction, Warszawer sought a haven in the labor camp in Wilga. He thought he might survive there. By the end of the second day, more than seventy Jews had been shot before his eyes. Among them was an adorable little girl; a German had first patted her on the head and then pressed that small head to the ground so that he could get better aim. Srul understood that he had to escape at once. He got out during the night and wandered the neighborhood, not knowing what to do. It was then that Smarzewski hid him.

Not long afterward it developed that some of the Jews from his town had been confined nearby in the town of Sobolew. The Germans announced that all those in hiding had a three-day grace period to go there, to the ghetto. When that time was up, both Jews and the Poles harboring them would be shot on the spot.

Srul led his boy to the ghetto, where he found his wife with his daughter and brother and sister. But he did not stay there permanently himself. In the ghetto, people were dropping in the street from hunger. By night, Warszawer wandered his old route among the villages and estates. He bought cattle, slaughtered it, and butchered it. Part he carried back to the ghetto, and part was smuggled to Warsaw, to be sold. He went to get his family on a certain Sunday in 1943 when he learned that within the next few days they were all to be transported to a death camp. He had come, but he would not be able to get out. Within an hour the Gestapo arrived and sealed the area.

Everyone was packed so tightly into cattle cars that they did not have room to move their hands even half an inch. People went mad from the heat and lack of air. When his son suffocated, nothing mattered to

Srul anymore. He smashed through the roof boards and broke out. Others followed. The Germans opened fire, and he threw himself to the ground, not moving. The train rolled away.

He does not remember how much time passed or how it passed. He dragged himself to Pielecki's house in the village of Przełek. Without a word, the peasant fed him and gave him something to drink, then spread a bundle of straw on the floor and covered Srul with a sheepskin coat. He lay there unconscious for four days. When he began to recover, he went to the next farmhouse, and then on—from neighbor to neighbor, village to village.

That was how the great wandering began. He always walked alone, because one man does not attract attention but two look suspicious. How did he stand it? Today he does not know how to explain. Neither does he know how to talk about what he lived through. He returns monotonously to a few images, a few stories.

"I was sitting at Paciorek's and eating breakfast and there a boy comes in, saying that the police are near the railroad tracks and they're approaching. Then I grabbed the scythe and the rake and pulled my cap down over my eyes and I went right at them. I went right across the tracks and into the rye and nobody stopped me.

"In Paweł Bozyk's barn that was in the field, five Jews made a hiding place for themselves. He didn't know about it. At night we'd meet in the woods and make a little fire and cook some food together. Somebody noticed once that we were sitting there, and then the Gestapo arrived and they surrounded the grove. And just then I had gone down to the stream to wash a shirt. I watched and I dug myself in under a spruce tree and they killed them by the fire.

"When they left I ran to Kornacica to Filipek's. He listened to everything and then at the break of day he ordered me to wait there and he went in to Sobolew himself. I didn't know why, but I was so exhausted that I just stayed there. And in three hours he came back. And he brought a loaf of bread. It was fresh and it smelled good. He gave it all to me and said, 'If I don't have bread I can cook something, but you can't do anything.' And he sent me to the barn for the whole night.

"Fourteen Jews had a hiding place dug in the ground in the woods. On top they put spruce trees so you couldn't see anything. They sat there a year and a half. Król the forester carried them food. Then, I don't know, he got scared or maybe they ran out of money, so he went and turned them in. The Germans came. They didn't even order them to come out. They killed them all with grenades in that hole. My brother was in there.

"In the village of Wielki Las the peasants came to me and they asked, what will you do if the police catch you? What if they ask where you get your food? And so I told them, I'll say I steal it at night. Anyway, I won't admit I get it from you. Am I stupid? And so then they decided that I had to make it; they decided that I had to survive."

"No one ever refused to help you?"

"No, not food! In twenty-six months, not once. Sometimes they were afraid to let me into the house, or into the barn. It varied, but their food they shared. And take Jarzabkowa, for instance, why, she was better than a rabbi's wife. To everybody who came, she gave—and a full bowl!"

"What did you do all day?"

"I didn't do anything. I walked around the woods, around the fields."

"Winter was the worst."

"No. In winter it was better. Nobody was snooping around the villages, and I generally had the woods to myself."

"Weren't you cold?"

"When I was, I ran."

"Weren't there times when you'd had enough?"

"There were. There were times when it got to me."

"And what then?"

"Nothing. I was indifferent. What will be, will be."

Warszawer lives next door to the shop. His daughter and her husband occupy the big room, and Zygmunt has the antechamber to the dark kitchen. His daughter has a television, phonograph, radio, sewing machine, and a suite of furniture; Zygmunt has a crooked wardrobe, a narrow bed, and a table. But on his walls hang large, garishly colored pictures: portraits of smiling children. The door to his daughter's room is never open, and when she goes out she locks it. In his little room Zygmunt almost always has guests—arrivals from back home surrounded by their luggage, or their children, already settled in the city mostly through Zygmunt's help.

He brought up his daughter himself when his wife left him. He married his wife after the war; she was a village girl, a Pole.

"Such a marriage before the war, oy, the community would have run me out of town!"

"How could you, a devout Jew, live with a Christian woman?"

"Those times when religion was big were gone. Of course I go to the synagogue on Saturdays, I keep all the holidays, but aside from that.... And with my wife, you know, it was the usual story. I prayed in the synagogue on Saturday and she prayed in the church on Sunday. And in general I'm open-minded. As long as a man's decent, his nationality is all the same."

"Did your wife's family feel the same way?"

"Right after the wedding my mother-in-law went to the priest to confess that she had a great burden on her heart because her daughter had married a Jew. And the priest said, 'Does he do anything wrong to her?' 'No,' my mother-in-law answered. 'Does he respect her?' 'Yes.' 'Does he allow her to go to church?' 'Yes.' 'Well, so what do you want?' And they got used to it."

"There's a lot of talk abroad about Polish anti-Semitism."

"In every country they blame the national minorities. Here the Jews, and in America the blacks. But after the war it was handled wrong. So many Jews signed up for the police and for the secret police. I would shout at them: Why are you doing this? What do you need it for? You want to beat people up and shoot people? So go to Israel. You want to be a colonel or something in the government? Do it in your own country with your own people, but not here. There's a handful of us left and still you're pushing."

"Why did so few Jews survive? Like down your way."

"How hard it was to survive, you don't have to tell me! But that wasn't the fault of the Poles, was it?"

"The Germans committed the crimes, of course, but some Poles robbed Jews and turned them in."

"Naturally, there were bad Poles, too. But were all the Jews good? In every nation there are swine and there are good people. I even met good Germans. Not many, but there were some. Like policeman Rym, he

always gave the Jews in the Sobolew ghetto the word when there was going to be a roundup."

"The majority of Jews left Poland."

"I was even happy to see the Jews leaving here after sixty-eight because otherwise everything would have been blamed on the Jews again."

"You stayed."

"I couldn't go away from here and leave those people who saved me. Maybe they will need me again, I thought. And they needed me.

"I couldn't go away from here and desert these people who saved me," Zygmunt-Srul Warszawer often repeats. Warszawer is shown during a visit to the home of Szymon Wiscnicki, who aided him during the war.

For years and years they've been sending their boys and girls here to me, to Warsaw. I look for work for them and send them to school. Even yesterday I found one of them a spot in a shop I know. I also did what I could for the old ones, supporting them in their poverty and misfortune. I'll even tell you that when they built a church in Łaskarzew, I donated money. And there isn't a wedding or a baptism they don't invite me to. Today when I arrive they're all happy because at least one survived, one exists."

Zygmunt paused and smiled. "In America I could have been a billionaire, but after all, money's not that important, and you can't buy everything, right?"

The outskirts of Łaskarzew. A settlement of small houses. Colorfully plastered, their yards are still not planted and they stand in mud. Among them, the occasional birch. The Jewish cemetery was here.

A monument stands in a clearing. It is a huge stone set on a concrete pedestal. On it a tablet reads:

O that my head were waters
And mine eyes a fountain of tears
That I might weep day and night
For the slain of the daughter of my people —Jeremiah 9, 1
To the Israelites of Łaskarzew and Sobolew,
murdered bestially in the years of annihilation 1939-1945.
Remember forever this horrible crime.
Eternal fame and eternal peace to their hallowed souls.
—Erected by Zygmunt Warszawer with the help of Franciszek Kopik

Autumn. I am walking along a village road with Zygmunt. Once again we are talking about the years gone by. I look at the flat, empty field and at the fragile forest in the distance and I think of the days and nights he spent here. I cannot help wondering aloud that in spite of it all he survived, he made it, he endured.

"And for what?" Warszawer starts unexpectedly. "So it can all be over with. And I'll be dead and buried."

"But forty years later."

Zygmunt does not answer; he walks slowly and looks off to the side. Then he raises his eyes to me and says seriously, "Oy, child, it's not such a big deal."

Zygmunt-Srul in his apartment.

CHAPTER FOUR

MY PRIVATE MADNESS

Poland is a country of paradoxes—this statement is often heard both from Poles and from foreigners visiting Poland. It is hard to deny the accuracy of the assessment. Here is a communist state in which more than 90 percent of the citizens are believing and practicing Catholics, and the number of churches is the highest in Europe. A police system prevails, yet hundreds of books and thousands of the most widely assorted types of periodicals, bulletins, and newspapers are published by secret presses beyond the reach of the censor and later turn up in almost every home. There are many such apparently irreconcilable contradictions in Poland. Without doubt another of them is the existence of a Jewish Theater performing in Yiddish in a country where there are no Jews. All the more so, since this is one of only two permanent Yiddish theaters in the world.

It is also a paradox that when there were still Jews in Poland this theater was located in a cramped, derelict old building. On rainy days washtubs were set among the audience to catch water dripping through the holes in the ceiling. Nevertheless, the house was always full. In 1971 the theater received a new home, large and contemporary. The hall contains more than three hundred seats, but during most performances the majority of them remain empty.

The manager of the theater and its artistic director is Szymon Szurmiej. Regardless of their opinion of him, everyone I spoke with agreed on one thing: if it were not for Szurmiej, there would be no Jewish Theater.

Szurmiej was born sixty-two years ago in Łuck, in the former

Szymon Szurmiej, in costume for "The Dybbuck," seated on the stage of his theater.

Polish eastern lands. His father was a Pole and an atheist and his mother a religious Jew, the daughter of a Chassid. She set the tone at home. She upheld tradition and observed all the holidays. Szymon went to *cheder* and then to a Polish *gimnazium*. This double identity was difficult. Poles called him a rotten Jew, and Jews nicknamed him *momzer*—"bastard." This made Szymon sensitive to all shadings of nationalism—Polish, Jewish, German—for the rest of his life.

During the war his father concealed his mother for two years. Then Ukranians denounced them and they both died. Szymon escaped to the USSR. There he survived the war and, after completing accelerated courses, became an actor. He returned to Poland in 1946 with a wife and a small son. They settled in Wrocław, in Lower Silesia. Szurmiej became a communist activist. He held assorted highly visible positions and was simultaneously an artist: a propoganda artist. What happened then—what he did then—is, as they say, a story in itself. In any case, he ceased active Party work in 1951. Then he began working in various Wrocław theaters; first as an actor, then as a literary adviser and finally as a director.

A few years later he acted under Ida Kamińska at the Jewish Theater for the first time. Afterward he went there often for guest appearances. He also led Jewish amateur groups in the provinces. When Ida left Poland after March, 1968, he took over the theater and has been running it ever since.

"Why is it that a Jewish theater exists in Poland?" I ask Szymon Szurmiej.

"Because that magnificent culture arose right here. And I am not thinking only of Yiddish works. Hebrew and Jewish culture cannot be separated, and it is a tragedy that particularly in Israel, this splendid limb has been lopped from the trunk. That leads only to impoverishment and decay, because Jewish culture is made up of the union of what is Hebrew and what is Yiddish. And that Jewish culture springs from right here. Jewish writing and learning, schooling and printing blossomed in unusually favorable circumstances in Poland over many centuries. A great literature arose here, in Hebrew and, later, above all in Yiddish, because that was the language of the nation, of those millions who had lived on Polish soil.

"A whole literature had its cradle in Poland: Mendel Mojcher Sforim, Shalom Aleichem, Shalom Asch, Jozef Opatushu, and many others. Even if they emigrated, they did not stop being writers from the Polish-Jewish milieu. Even Isaac Bashevis Singer, who won the Nobel Prize, was born in Radzymin near Warsaw. He has lived in the States for fifty years, and for fifty years he has gone on describing an unchanging world of Polish Jews— the world that shaped him."

"Except that such a world no longer exists."

"So there is all the more reason to show it, remember it, resurrect it. That is what our theater does. And we can do it! Staging literary masterpieces does not pay. And here we have the second part of the answer to the question about why this theater is active in Poland. It is active because the state gives us money—big money, fifty million złoty a year. Joint* also helps. Thanks to that I can put on what is most valuable

*Joint—The Joint Distribution Company (JDC) is the largest Jewish aid organization in Poland, dating from 1914. Technical and financial aid from Joint extends to most major Jewish organizations in Poland. Joint also distributes individual material assistance to about five thousand people. These are mostly Jews, but also include a certain number of Poles who helped to save Jewish lives during the war.

in Jewish literature without worrying about the box office and without pandering to cheap tastes."

"Jewish theater has a very rich tradition here."

"Enormous. The first Jewish play, *The Messiah* opened in Warsaw in 1837. Jewish theater flourished here over the next hundred years. In 1939 there were fifteen permanent professional companies and several dozen traveling theaters. There were even theatres in the Warsaw Ghetto, and then there was a Yiddish-language performance in Lublin immediately after the liberation in 1944."

"Many people have doubts about performing in a cemetery."

"But it was necessary to drive away the death that surviving Jews carried in themselves along with the memories of the murdered, the asphyxiated, the ones who were shot. It was necessary to free them from their nightmares so that they could go on living. The words of the prophets are appropriate: 'Comfort my people, because they need comfort.' And it was precisely the living Jewish word that became such a comfort. The actress Diana Blumenfeld came to Lublin. Standing on legs that were still swollen, dressed in a wine-red housecoat, she sang Jewish songs at the first concert in the house of Peretz. Not long afterward there was a concert at the municipal theater. The hall was packed with people who one day earlier had had no right to live. Something mystical seemed to be happening. Diana had managed to enunciate only the first words when the whole audience broke out in powerful sobbing. It was a great catharsis. That concert became the beginning of a new Jewish theater born after the days of the deluge. And then it all broke loose like an avalanche. Wherever Jews turned up, artistic groups, often composed exclusively of amateurs, arose. At the same time large, fully professional theaters were created in Łódż and Wrocław. In 1950 they were joined in the Ester Rachel Kamińska State Jewish Theater. It has now been going for thirty-five years. This year we have our anniversary."

"Yes, but during those years the situation has changed radically. Jews have emigrated from Poland. But the theater has remained."

"First of all, not everyone left. Only a few stayed, but precisely those who needed us most. You have traveled around Poland with the theater many times and have seen how these old, predominantly lonely, often sick people received us, with what emotion and open-heartedness. To them we are the only entertainment and often the only solace. Such appearances are part of our everyday work. The theater has two stages, as it were: the permanent one in Warsaw and a movable one in the fourteen cities where there are active Jewish clubs."

"These old people are your best audience. They are the last ones who still understand Yiddish, because most of the Jews in Warsaw are completely assimilated. Just like Poles, they have to listen to a simultaneous translation of the performance through headphones. Isn't such playing to the headphones depressing for the actors?"

"Naturally we prefer it when someone reacts directly, and the actors always look carefully to see if there is someone without headphones. If there is, they point him out to each other and they are happy that there is at least one person who understands. But playing to that audience in headphones is also very satisfying. Especially because we have many faithful viewers among them."

"Poles as well?'

"Of course. Jewish culture is, after all, part of Polish culture. For many centuries they developed together and intermingled. There are many works in both languages that reflect the mutual influence. Many prominent Polish poets come from Jewish families. Many Jewish artists had Polish friends."

"In your version the life of Jews in Poland sounds idyllic."

"It was no idyll. It had its dark sides—many, in fact—but also bright sides, radiant—the great development of Jewish culture, learning, and language. The source was here. Now I want to mention the third dimension of our existence: the external dimension. Because our theater is not only for Poland. We play for Jews living in various parts of the world—in Israel, in America, in western Europe. And they receive us everywhere with exceptional warmth. For various reasons. Old emigres long for the world of their youth and find it in us. Young Jews are looking for their roots, and all roots lead right here."

"Why aren't there any permanent theaters in the world that perform in Yiddish? Even in the United States?"

"There were excellent theaters in America during the great influx of Jewish immigration. But after a few dozen years they went into a decline until they disappeared, collapsing entirely."

"But why? After all, there are five million Jews there—more than in Israel."

"That is a complex problem. Jewish culture is a plebian culture.

Jews who moved up in society in the United States became assimilated into the English-speaking culture and were often ashamed of their simple origins. It was only the next generation that began to seek its national identity. And then again, the American theater developed and keeps developing all the time, while the Jewish theater stood still. In practice this meant going backward, regressing, and more and more of a ghetto mentality. The lack of patrons meant that the repertoire became more commercial and was performed on a lower and lower level, until in the end there were only small groups active in the States, without permanent homes. They would spring up to perform one play, usually a boulevard melodrama. Jews called it *shunt*—"trash."

"What happened to all the leading actors who left Poland?"

"Some of them managed to have careers. Unfortunately, they are exceptions. The most outstanding dramatic actors went mostly to the Hebrew theaters in Israel or the English ones in the U.S. But the language barrier was so great that few managed to make the switch. Ida Kamińska directed our theater until 1968, and she was an unusually popular figure. She told us during a meeting in Israel, nine years after she emigrated, 'If you want to be Jewish actors, don't leave Poland.'"

"You took over the theater in 1970."

"Then, after the great emigration of 1968, the theater was in complete disarray. There were no more than seven actors left. I had to build everything from scratch—the company, the repertoire. But the most important problem was giving back to people a faith in the sense of their work. They had to believe not only that the theater was alive but that it was going to develop further."

"How did you manage to do it?"

"It was necessary to attract people—above all young people. I founded a youth studio in the theater that trains actors and at the same time teaches them Jewish history and literature as well as the Yiddish language. In the course of fifteen years, scores of people have gone through that studio. Many of them act in our theater."

"But the majority have left."

"That's right, but we keep recruiting new ones."

"What is the theater like today?"

"In the sense of a group: young, which pleases me greatly. Of course we have an older contingent, very experienced actors who were already active in Jewish theaters before the war. The most outstanding among them is Michał Szwejlich. But the future belongs to the young."

"There is a widespread opinion that it is almost entirely Poles who act in the Jewish Theater."

"That's not true. All our old actors are Jews, and a large percentage of the younger ones. But such talk simply drives me into a fury. It's an obsession, particularly among foreign Jews. They don't ask me about the artistic profile of the theater or the quality of the performances, but only about the birth certificates of the actors. I would understand if they accused me of faking, of making a colorful parrot out of a dung bird, but no! They are only interested in how many *goyim* I have in the company. When we appeared in Israel I ran into so much of that that in the town of Petah Tikva I came out onstage before the curtain went up and said, 'I want to tell you a legend about Baal Shem Tov, a great wise man, the creator of Chassidism. It is *Yom Kippur*, but it is impossible to finish because the Lord God has become offended with the Jews and closed heaven. Baal Shem Tov enters into a dispute with God and tries to persuade Him to forgive the Jews. Without effect, however. In the prayer house despair and grief prevail. The Jews are weeping, moaning, and some of them exhausted by fasting, faint. In the middle of all this the *shabbes goy* arrives to put out the candles. Amazed, he asks why they are sobbing so terribly. When they tell him that it is because the Lord God is offended, the boy says, "I don't know how to pray your way because I'm a *goy*, but I can whistle. Maybe that will help." And he whistles so loud that God laughs and opens heaven. So I tell you, if you find one *goy* who whistles and in that way contributes to the development of Jewish culture, I will kiss his hand.' There was applause and they gave me peace on that theme."

"Why, according to you, do young people come to this theater? Because of a love of Jewish culture?"

"It varies. For young Jews, coming predominantly from assimilated families, it is a chance to return to their Jewishness, an opportunity to become acquainted with the culture and traditions of their people. Many Poles, on the other hand, are fascinated by the exotica that the culture of Polish Jews represents to them. And this is sometimes transformed into the passion of a lifetime. Our actress Wanda Siemaszko not only learned Yiddish fluently but is finishing a university degree in Hebrew."

"I think, however, that there are also some for whom this is simply the easiest road to the theater. It's easy to get into your theater, and very hard to get into drama school."

"That's true. Recently one of our apprentices even told me that she would learn Chinese if it gave her a chance to act."

"Now let's talk about you. At this moment you are a man and an institution. You fill many political and public functions, you appear on television for various official occasions, and recently you have even been a candidate for parliament. This is unpopular in Poland, especially since the introduction of martial law when the universal reaction of society was boycotts—a boycott of the authorities, of official positions, of television appearances, and so on. You are a figure who evokes mixed feelings, among Jews as well as non-Jews. You know this."

"I know it, but it concerns me as much, it hurts me as much, as if I were lame and a dog bit me in my artificial leg. You see, I am a prosthesis, because in fact I am not here. I do not exist."

"What does that mean?"

"That means that if I have lived through the annihilation of my people, if all the things with which I was raised have gone up the chimneys, I am already somehow on the other side. I have only one passion left: to protect the flame that has survived. It never even enters my mind that this culture could go away, disappear, that it could be reduced to ashes and old photographs. I am ready to do everything for it to survive."

"I have always known who I am," says Golda Tencer, the star of the Jewish Theater. "For other young people our theater is a return to Jewishness, but I am not returning because I never left."

"Do you believe that you will succeed?"

"I believe that."

"Mr. Szurmiej, I think that you want very much to believe."

"Well, I admit that I sometimes have doubts. Then I think that aside from Schwejlich, who knows this culture the way I do, it no longer matters to anyone else. I feel very lonely, like the last one... Perhaps what I am doing is quixotic. But after all, in 1939 there were sixteen million

people all around the world who spoke Yiddish. Hitler smothered the source, but all the same there is still living sap in this tree. And that is exactly what I want to communicate. American Jews have no cultural identity. Israel is aggressive politically but not culturally, because what it has to offer is still too young. And it is precisely my idea to communicate this vast, old heritage to all of them. This transcends political systems, all barriers. In the Bible it is beautifully formulated: Who saves one life, saves mankind. It is the same here: who saves a culture ... And besides, this is such a culture, there is not another one like it in the world. It is impregnated with blood and tears. It has cost too much to disappear for good. This may be my private madness, but it is the way I see it."

"These old, often lonely people are our best audience," say the actors of the Jewish Theater about the viewers of their road shows. "To them we are the only entertainment and often the only solace." Juliusz Berger, one of the principal actors of the Theater, is shown during a performance in the Jewish club in Gliwice, attended by the majority of the Jews residing in the city.

Portraits of the audience at a Jewish Theater touring performances.

Preceding page: "I play in a mask because the director wanted me to, but at the same time this is a scene that eminently symbolizes the situation of Jews in Poland. Real Jews barely exist anymore. In their place remain masks, pictures, photographs..." says Marek Weglarski, a Jewish Theater actor.

The Fiddler on the Roof of the Palace of Culture and Science in Warsaw, where there was a performance of the famous musical. For most Poles, the Palace of Culture and Science, erected by the Russians in 1955, is a symbol of the new, communist Poland and of its subjugation to the USSR.

CHAPTER FIVE

THE COMMUNITY

"The Jews in Poland are a nation that is departing but not arriving," said Moses Finkelstein, the president of the Congregation of the Mosaic Faith. His congregation has eighteen hundred members throughout the country, and it is constantly growing smaller. Several dozen people die each year, while no one joins.

There are congregations in fifteen cities. The smallest have little more than a dozen members. The largest is found in Kraków. In mid-1985, the congregation there numbered 204 people. Average age: sixty-nine.

The congregation building, the same one as before the war, stands on Skawinska Street in the center of Kazimierz, the former Jewish quarter. Massive, four stories high, with extensive cellars, it served exclusively the more than sixty-thousand Kraków Jews who belonged to the community until 1939. Its functional modernity combined with rather ostentatious richness mirrored the wealth and power of the local Jewish society of those times.

Wide marble stairs led to the top floor, where a meeting hall with crystal chandeliers, leather-covered furniture, and high ceilings was located. Weddings were also performed there. The lower stories were filled with numerous offices and archives, and the basement contained a splendidly equipped gymnasium. After the war the Jewish garment cooperative restored the devastated building. The congregation received one story. Poles later took over the cooperative because the Jews were leaving or retiring. The congregation contracted. Now it uses only part of the cellars and half of the third floor, where a small office, a kitchen, a food storeroom, and a cafeteria are located.

It is usually empty. Only in the afternoon do people—about thirty of them—appear. They arrive singly; old, bent over, often leaning on canes. They sit at the oilcloth-covered table and slowly, seriously eat their free kosher dinners. These are a gift from Joint, which sends the cans, concentrates, and powders necessary for preparing the meals. Many more people who live far from the congregation building would like to take advantage of the dinners, but such a journey every day would be too much for them. Yet they always gather here for the *seder* supper.

This is the one night in the year when the modest room takes on life and sparkle. The tables are arranged in a horseshoe pattern and covered with white tablecloths. They are set with a holiday service; with candleholders and lighted candles, heaps of matzo sent from Hungary, and bottles of sweet Israeli wine. During the *Pesach* holiday as well, the Kraków community is noisy and festive. Delicious, fragrant *seder* dishes cooked home-style are served instead of canned food. The man sitting beside me says with gentle melancholy, "Just a little bit like it used to be..."

The banqueters are dressed *en fete*, with Old World elegance. Not a single young face can be seen; except that at the end of the table, under a window, a girl and two boys are sitting. These are American students, Jews, in Kraków over the holiday. At first everyone gathered around them. When it turned out, however, that they did not know Yiddish, it ended in smiles and hearty claps on the back. And so once again there is no one from the younger generation to ask, according to tradition and in the words of the *Haggadah*: "Why is this evening different from all other evenings?"

Somewhat earlier, during the holiday prayers in the Remu synagogue, the men quarreled. First there were nervous whispers from the direction of the *bimah* and then the voices grew more distinct until the exchanges, all in Yiddish, turned into a loud argument. Five old men in *tallises* crowded close together. They waved their prayerbooks in violent gestures. The rest of those present looked on in silence.

"Everybody wants to say a different prayer," Czesław Jakubowicz, the president of the community, explained to me. After a moment he added, "I could feel it coming to this. There's no one left in Kraków who knows how to pray."

"Couldn't you settle it?" I asked.

Jakubowicz shook his head. "How, since I don't know either?"

A year ago the Kraków Jews still prayed in two synagogues. There was even a division between the more Orthodox and the more Reformed, although it was difficult to be precise about exactly what that meant. The former belonged to the small, historic prayer house named after its founder, the eminent sixteenth-century Talmudist, philosopher and historian Mojzesz Isserles, known as Remu. The latter gathered in the Templum. That spacious synagogue, with its wooden interior decorated with unique polychromatic bas reliefs, was led before the war by the well-known reformer, rabbi, and member of parliament Ozjasz Thon.

After the war, the rabbis who had survived the Holocaust dispersed around the world. The last one left Poland in 1970. Since then devout Jews have been left to their own devices. For many years the prayers were led in Kraków by two very religious and universally respected people, Abram Fogel in Remu and Abram Lesman in the Templum.

Both are dead now. They died several months ago, one after the other, and together with them, as some say, Jewishness died in Kraków. Yet several hundred Jews still live here, and it is they, even if they sometimes feel helpless and abandoned, even if many of them have completely departed from the rules of the Law and the remainder have trouble praying, who constitute the greatest Jewish community in Poland; many say the only one and the last one. And this is so despite the fact that more or less the same number of Jews live in Warsaw or Wrocław as in Kraków. After all, it is not a matter of dry statistics but of living bonds among people, of preserving continuity with what once was, of tradition. This is what distinguishes Kraków.

Kraków has long been a conservative city, and its inhabitants, little inclined to rapid change, attach great importance to the past. This acquired particular significance after the Second World War, when genuine migrations of people began in Poland. The borders of the country had been changed radically, the majority of the cities lay in ruins, the villages were ravaged and depopulated. This all caused a redistribution and complete intermingling of populations, to which Kraków was one of the few exceptions. It survived in a physical and, at least partially, in a spiritual sense because the social, family, and community bonds were not completely torn apart here.

This also had great significance for the local Jews. In fact, the Holocaust did not pass over the Kraków Jews, but those who survived and those who came afterward melted together in the favorable atmosphere to form a new community. It was also important that the Kazimierz district contained an unusually large number of Jewish monuments. They survived the war, while the Jewish district of Warsaw, together with the rest of the city, was literally razed to the ground. Kraków's Jews could thus find their identity more easily.

So it happened. The community here was unusually lively and active after the war. The significant numbers of intelligentsia, people with higher education and often with solid academic or artistic credentials, was also exceptional. There were more than six thousand Jews in Kraków in 1945. Sucessive emigrations diminished this figure. Today there are approximately five hundred of them in the whole city: the devout and the nonreligious, a tiny group, a tiny community. And at the same time, preeminent.

Róża Jakubowicz is mother to the community. Her husband Meir led the Kraków congregation for nearly thirty years. The Jakubowicz clan still leads it. The current president, Czesław, became the successor to his uncle, Meir.

Róża is an unusual person. Seventy, in poor health, she never holds anything back and is always ready to work for the community, to help those who need her.

"Ach, the Jews of Kraków..." she says to me with a sigh. "I knew them in their days of splendor. Then they were murdered before my eyes.

After the war they existed for a moment, but now it's over, twilight. So I want them to have it as good as they can in these last moments."

It is she who, with only one kitchen helper, prepares the annual *seder* specialties for several dozen people, while in other communities in Poland they are opening cans sent by Joint for the occasion. It is she, the last one in Kraków, who bakes real *challahs* at home for special occasions. She embroidered seven *Torah* mantles and offered them to Tempel and Remu synagogues. The list could go on and on.

The most important thing, however, is the atmosphere that Róża creates in the Kraków community. "You can feel a woman's touch here," visiting Jews from other parts of the country say with envy. Róża is always serene, full of optimism, and cheerful.

"To tell the truth, I don't know myself where it comes from," she told me once. "During the war I lost twenty-seven close relatives. I lost everything I possessed—my fortune, my position, my house. A whole world, the Jewish world, which I loved and in which I grew up, disappeared. And I still manage to smile. Oy, a person can take a lot."

Róża comes from a wealthy family. Her father had a large tannery that supplied the army. There were five sisters and three brothers. Róża, the youngest, graduated from the Commercial School in order to be able to help her beloved father as an accountant. Her husband's family also belonged to the Jewish plutocracy. The Jakubowiczes came from Wadowice, where Róża's father-in-law owned the largest and most modern synthetic fertilizer factory in Poland. Immediately after the beginning of the war, the Germans began producing parts for their V-1 and V-2

Róża Jakubowicz, "the mother of the community," serving a dish she has prepared for the seder *supper.*

superweapons there.

Róża's son Tadeusz was born in 1939. He was an unusually beautiful child; therefore, when the anti-Jewish terror began to intensify, a Polish friend offered to adopt him and bring him up as her own. "I couldn't bring myself to do it," says Róża. "I cried whole nights, until in the end I decided to keep him. What would happen to me would happen to him."

Róża saved little Tadeusz, along with eight other people. That was after the partial liquidation of the ghetto, in which the majority of her family perished. The Jakubowiczes escaped to the forest. On hilly land far from any settlement, they built a shelter. "Today people say, 'You lived in a bunker,' and they imagine a comfortable shed." Róża shakes her head. "But it was a den dug into the ground, and you crawled in on your belly. It was a grave in which we spent three years."

The worst problem was finding food. The only person who could leave the forest was Róża. She had Aryan papers and, most importantly, an Aryan appearance. She would walk to Kraków, buy food, and return alone, on foot. With one difference: on they way back she carried a sack over her shoulder. Under normal conditions she would not have been able to budge it an inch. But now she trudged thirty miles under its enormous weight.

At the foot of the hillock where the hiding place was situated, she would hide the sack in the bushes and go to inform those who were waiting. Three men would then carry it to the top.

"And often," as one of them, Czesław Jakubowicz, remembers, "we could not move it. To this day I go around wondering how you did it."

"So do I," says Róża with a smile. "And remember, Czesław, how it poured rain a couple of nights ago? I told you, 'If you offered me a thousand dollars to spend that one night in the woods, I'd turn you down without even thinking about it.' And back then it was raining and snowing and freezing and we thanked God for making it through one more day."

When I ask Róża about what she has done for the community and the Jews of Kraków during the forty postwar years, she dodges the question. "I did what had to be done. It's good I had the strength." Then she adds, "My Tadeusz is really a good boy. He dedicates himself to these old people. Write about him."

Róża is not exaggerating out of maternal fondness. Tadeusz Jakubowicz, a man in the prime of life, has no private existence. His divorced wife and beloved daughter have moved to another city. He did not remarry. Outside work, all his time is marked for looking after the ill and the lonely—which means the majority of the Kraków community. Tadeusz is friend, confidant, and nursemaid to them.

Ceaselessly preoccupied with his charges, he is in constant motion. He arranges a hospital bed for one, shops for a second, and makes three visits a day to a third who is in a nursing home and will accept meals from no one else. Jakubowicz consults with doctors, accompanies the old people even in their death agonies, comforts the families, and often organizes the funerals as well.

"Why do you do it?" I ask him.

Tadeusz, a reticent and shy man, thinks for a long moment and then replies, "I like old people."

"When did you begin taking care of them?"

"A long time ago, more than ten years ago."

"How did you get started?"

"Oh, simply... somebody needed something, so Tadeusz would do it. It went from there."

"Do other younger members of the community also help?"

"Well, not much. Once a lady, a music teacher, came to me and asked what sort of funds there were for those who helped the old people. That got me so upset I almost kicked her down the stairs. There are others, too, who think only of money. Preferably dollars."

"Of course you receive no compensation."

"Fortunately, we do well. We have a shop that produces veneer. Because, to tell the truth, it costs me money, but as long as I have it, I don't worry about it."

"Doesn't it wear you out?"

"What?"

"Constantly being with old, sick people."

"And why should that wear me out? I don't understand."

Tadeusz Jakubowicz in the kitchen of his family home in Wadowice.

The president of the congregation occupies a small, modest room. Pictures of prewar Kraków and portraits of early rabbis hang on the walls. A nineteenth-century *Torah* crown holds the place of honor. Czesław Jakubowicz rarely sits behind his massive desk. He tends to move around, talking to people. His Uncle Meir, who died in 1979, was an energetic, authoritative, and rather inaccessible man. Czesław is less resourceful, less educated, but, as they say in the community, "a *mensch*."

"Why did you become president?" I ask.

"Well, they picked me. And why? It had a little to do with family tradition, and my uncle, but above all I was the youngest of these old people, healthier than them, strong. But I wasn't looking for the job."

"But it is an honor, Mr. Jakubowicz."

"Sure, it's an honor to lead a congregation with a tradition like ours, and also a satisfaction that I can do something for people. Because they truly need help. But from day to day it is mainly work and nerves."

"Nerves? Why?"

"The people are not easy. Not that I don't understand. They're old, ailing, and they've been through a lot. I often have to keep the peace because they argue and become offended. There are so few of us; why can't we live in harmony?"

"What do they argue about?"

"Trifles, like children."

"Recently about prayers."

"That's another matter, and very serious. We have to give up praying in one of the synagogues and come together in the other one.

And yet I have no one who can lead us in prayer."

"In all of Kraków you cannot find one truly devout man?"

"Among the two hundred members of the congregation, women predominate, because it was easier for them to survive the war. These few men, now, are actually attached to tradition, but they have no religious training or else they've forgotten it all. This or that one might even know how to read the book, but he won't know what he's reading. He doesn't understand."

"And you?"

"I'm a good example of that semi-illiteracy. I grew up in a pious family, I went to Hebrew *gimnazium*, and then I forgot everything."

"So what will you do?"

"Well, we are not going to stop praying, even though it's certain that not everything will be correct."

"Money always arouses the greatest passions, especially the money of Jews—even of a handful of old people, like here in Kraków. Myths are current around town about the wealth of both individuals and of the Jewish community."

"Those are nothing but myths. Here's the truth: Joint, augmented by other Jewish organizations, supports us. Those are mostly central organizations, through Warsaw. Besides money for community activities we receive kosher food, medicine, and grants in aid for individual members."

"Are those big sums?"

"They irritate people because they are in dollars."

"The dollar is a symbol of wealth here."

"That's right. But our members hardly receive astronomical sums. Only, depending on their means, from two to six checks a year, each for around forty dollars. I'll grant that, in Poland, that's something. I think, though, that this myth about wealth comes from the fact that some of the Jews in Kraków are simply rich. Thanks to their own work, as doctors or lawyers, or help from relatives abroad. Sometimes it only comes out after

they die. A man lives modestly, and then it turns out that he deposited dollars in an account and the bank is looking for heirs. But they usually don't find any."

"And the money is forfeited."

"It goes to the state treasury. There have even been suggestions among us that if someone is alone, he should will the money to the congregation. Then we might be able to renovate the synagogue or the cemetery. But I've never urged anyone to do that, because everybody should be able to do what he likes with his money."

"Has anyone done it?"

"So far, no."

"And so none of you suffers from poverty?"

"No. What's more, we've lately had a couple pretending to be destitute."

"Why?"

"To swindle money out of tourists: Jews who come here mainly from the U.S. These ones of ours come up to them and say they have nothing to live on. One even takes out his false teeth, hides them in his pocket, and shows his bare gums, saying that he can't afford to go to the dentist. They demand dollars."

A fragment of the garden square in front of the Templum synagogue in the Kazimierz district of Kraków. The doors lead to the mikvah, *the ritual baths—the last in Poland. On the bench, in the middle, sits Czesław Jakubowicz, the president of the Kraków Jewish congregation.*

"They ask, perhaps."

"No, they insist. They say: 'You're rich. You have to share with us.'"

"Not exactly elegant."

"I am appalled. This is really marginal—three or four people—but they disgrace the whole community and after all, we really have solid, honest people here."

"Why do they do it?"

"Miss Niezabitowska, it's not all pearls among Jews, either."

"I know that the tourists who visit you are otherwise very eager to help—not so much to give to beggars as to offer something for the community or for saving the Jewish monuments, of which there are so many in Krakow."

"That is very true. These are sometimes very wealthy people. They want to give us something to help. They often tell me, 'Just let us know what you want.'"

"And how do you answer?"

"I answer them in the words of my Aunt Róża: 'Bring us youth, joy, life... That is what we really miss.'"

In the Kazimierz district of Kraków, the so-called Jewish Town, there are no Jews.

I am walking along Jósef Street, once the major artery of the quarter, with Wiktor Traubman, who was born here eighty-five years ago and has spent his whole life in Kraków. A few minutes ago, when we entered Kazimierz, Wiktor told me, "No one else could talk me into this, daughter. I never walk here. If I'm going for prayers, this is the shortest way from the streetcar to the synagogue and back. But nobody who saw Kazimierz before the war—even once—can walk in peace through this cemetery."

Even today, on a fair spring day forty years after the war, this place seems dead. Old, dilapidated houses with damp streaked walls, some of them in complete ruin, stand along the narrow streets. The windows are mostly dirty and empty, without curtains, lights, or flowers. Some are smashed out, some boarded up.

Kazimierz is dying for the second time. During the war the Germans deported all its inhabitants to the ghetto. They left the houses. Now the centuries-old buildings, long unrenovated, are falling apart on their own.

Jews lived in Kazimierz for five hundred years. Surrounded by walls, they created their own world here. Even when they were free to settle anywhere in the city after the lifting of restrictions in the middle of the nineteenth century, Kazimierz remained their place—the place where religious, scholarly, political, and cultural life was concentrated, and where it flourished. 304 prayer houses, among them many synagogues of great architectural value, along with dozens of active secular and talmudic schools, all sorts of associations and organizations, sports club, theaters, and cabarets existed in Kraków in 1939.

Wiktor Traubman was, as he says of himself, "an average Jew, one of the thousands who created the world of Kazimierz." Neither poor nor rich, he owned a tin shop, worked hard, and honestly made enough money to keep his family. He was also active in the Jewish trade unions,

but his greatest passion was sports.

For many years he boxed with the Maccabees, the most famous Jewish sports club, which fielded teams in more than a dozen disciplines. Jewish youth trained with great enthusiasm and considerable success. "There was a joke going around Kraków," Wiktor tells me. "Two Polish fans are talking after watching the Maccabees defeat the 'Aryan' Wisła club in a soccer match. One says, 'I'm not at all anti-Semitic. Hebrew teams are okay with me—but why should they have Jews playing for them?' "

Wiktor believes that his good physical condition and the inner discipline that he developed in himself over many years of training helped him greatly in surviving the war. Along with a feeling of self-respect. "Remember, child," he explains emphatically, "you have to preserve that—or at least try to do it, even in the most terrible conditions—because enemies always try first of all to destroy your pride and conviction of your own worth." And Wiktor Traubman, the tinsmith, recites a fragment of Heine to me in beautiful German:

Hold up your head
Even when threatened,
Fight for your just piece of bread
And never be degraded to a flunkey's role
Guard your human rights.

When he finishes, he nods and adds, "That helped me, helped me a great deal indeed."

Wiktor Traubman, 85, in his home.

During the war Wiktor shared the fate of the majority of the Kraków Jews. Together with his family, he was confined in the newly created Podgorze ghetto in March, 1941. There, during the second successive liquidation, the Germans murdered Wiktor's mother, wife, and two daughters before his eyes on Wednesday, October 28, 1942. Wiktor has told about it many times, as if speaking about this unspeakable tragedy and crying in the presence of a sympathetic person brings him at least moments of relief.

Wiktor married again, but he has no children. He and his wife never mention the war. Traubman met her in 1946 and decided to take care of her, a woman in a state of deep depression. During the war she and her son were picked up on the street and, despite her Aryan papers, it was discovered that they were Jews. One of the soldiers, named Schubke, drew his pistol and shot the child the woman was holding in her arms. Schubke was apprehended after the war, brought to Kraków, and sentenced to death on the evidence of, among others, Helena Traubman. But she was never herself again.

Wiktor, as he says, managed to survive "that great hunt for live animals branded with the yellow patch." After the final destruction of the ghetto, the Kraków Jews who remained alive were transferred to a new camp he helped build in Płaszow. He survived the destruction of that camp as well and went with a column of prisoners to Auschwitz. From there, in one of the last transports, he was sent to Sachsenhausen in January, 1945. Dressed only in their striped camp "pajamas," they rode fourteen days in open trucks. The majority froze along the way. He was freed on the last day of the war, May 8, by a Polish unit fighting among the Allied armies. He weighed eighty pounds.

Wiktor returned to Kraków, but not to Kazimierz. He did not even want to see it. "I haven't walked here the way I'm walking with you for forty-some years, daughter," he says today. But he has forgotten nothing. Many of the streets we wander through are several hundred years old. Wiktor narrates and comments. And all the time one phrase repeats itself: used to be, used to be, used to be. Here used to be the *tallis* maker's, there used to be the shop of cross-eyed Abramek who courted his sister, next door used to be the *beit midrash* school....

We enter the courtyards and sometimes the buildings. Some are occupied, but the postwar tenants of most of them have been moved to new districts of the city. Of the earlier residents there remain principally the names of the streets—Izaak, Ester, Jakub—and, very rarely, a surprising trace: the recess on a door where there was once a *mezuzah*; a Hebrew sign showing through where the plaster is falling away.

In the Kazimierz district of Kraków, the so-called Jewish Town, there are no Jews.

Attorney Mauricy Wiener loves Kraków very much. During the war, during his six years in the USSR, hardly a night passed when he did not dream of the moment of his return. Now, when he comes back from his frequent luxurious journeys to various western European countries, he feels, as he defines it, "great joy at getting back to this garbage can."

Kraków has long ceased to be the beautiful little town of his youth, an architectural knicknack set among green hills. Chaotic postwar development, poisonous soot from nearby factories, an excess of automobiles, and a lack of cleanliness have changed the city. But to Mauricy Wiener and his wife Janina, Kraków—even gray, decaying, and neglected—is still their city.

It is not, however, the Kraków of Wiktor Traubman. It is a Kraków of stylish turn-of-the-century townhouses, wide streets and promenades through flourishing parks; the Kraków of the Jewish intelligentsia who, emancipating themselves before the war from the ghetto of Kazimierz, created together with the Poles an intellectual elite. University professors, composers, and stage artists, famous lawyers and sought-after doctors led a stable, colorful life here. Their reminiscences are full of stories of soirees, gala performances at the opera, and carefree excursions to the nearby Tatras. A part of this milieu survived the war. In altered circumstances they created a new style of life, which nevertheless preserved much of their former habits and something of the bygone splendor.

Wiener was born in Kraków in 1906. "My grandfather" he tells me, "was very devout. He wore a *challat*, sidecurls, and lived strictly according to the severe rules of the Law in a closed Jewish environment. My father was Reformed. He dressed in secular clothes, spent a good deal of time among Poles, but at home observed the traditions. As for me, in the fifteenth year of my life I renounced the Covenant with the Lord and to this day have not resumed any contact with Him."

At the age of fifteen Mauricy joined the Communist Youth League. He was never much of an activist, rather a constant supporter. Today he says with distance, "Once I looked with faith and hope upon the new order that was introduced here, and later only with indulgence."

Immediately upon the end of the war, attorney Wiener began working in the Jewish Committee. He was its vice president, and from 1957 on he has been the chairman of the Kraków branch of the Jewish Social-Cultural Association.

"It was a splendid environment," he recalls. "Even after the war, Kraków was a city of intellectuals, and the Jewish intelligentsia stood in the vanguard. During the great emigration of 1968, approximately two thousand directors, actors, journalists, writers, doctors, and lawyers alone left here."

"What is it like now?" I ask.

"Much worse, of course. Above all there are far, far fewer of us. One of my friends made a list of names and he came up with five hundred and twenty Jews in Kraków, among whom intellectuals still predominate, but after all, that is a trifling figure when set against the half-million inhabitants of the city."

"Do you know all of them?"

Mauricy and Janina Wiener at home.

"At best by sight, but there is a smaller group of us that sticks together. We have our club, in which quite a bit happens, but mostly we meet privately. And that is what makes life in Kraków so interesting—the people we have made friends with, and the places we visit together. One of our friends, a dentist, emigrated to Sweden. He did well there. He had a life of luxury, but he returned because he was very bored."

"That might be the only case in the history of this country."

"You may laugh. Of course, when people leave they usually burn their bridges behind them, but that does not change the fact that you cannot be bored in Kraków. Something interesting is always happening here. We have performances, exhibitions, concerts on the highest European level. And then the meetings, the parties..."

"I have attended several such evenings. For us, as residents of other cities, it is a jarring experience: vast, beautiful apartments furnished with antiques, the walls hung with masterpieces, elegant meals on eighteenth-century porcelain. I think these are the last salons in this part of the world, between Berlin and Vladivostok."

"But these are not only Jewish salons."

"I was hardly suggesting that. I am rather thinking of a certain style."

"The style is indeed unique. And if we are to speak of the milieu, it is not, God forbid, closed. We have no quotas. We also have our Polish friends."

"And do Poles make friends with you?"

"Naturally. This is a matter of personal sympathies, and not of national divisions."

"Is there no more anti-Semitism in Kraków?"

"Occasionally someone will write *Jude-Schweine!* on the wall of the building where our club is located. But we rather suspect Arabs, of whom there are many in town, of the authorship."

"And is that all?"

"Things have changed greatly. I remember coming back from the USSR in 1945 with a group of Jewish children. I had run an orphanage in Turkestan. We returned by train. As soon as we entered Poland, it began. At the stations they spat on us and shouted, 'What are you doing here, oven fodder?' The children were shocked. So was I. There was a particularly anti-Semitic mood then, a poisonous atmosphere."

"And now?"

"The older ones have, well, calmed down. The younger generation, on the other hand, is splendid. Lately I have again had several meetings with students. They invite me to talk about Jewish culture. The nationalistic feelings have been completely distilled out of them. There is no anti-Semitism in them. On the contrary, I often encounter signs of interest in and sympathy toward Jews. There is only one problem..."

"What?"

"The fact that in Poland there is no longer, unfortunately, any object for that sympathy. The Poles were a little tardy."

Besides the Jewish Theater, the only place in Poland offering Yiddish lessons is the Kraków Jewish Social-Cultural Association. Six or seven people come once a week for two hours of lessons. Among them are only two Jews: one of the students, and the teacher.

The teacher does not want me to reveal his name. A handsome, elegant man of around sixty, he greets me with a friendly smile. He will talk willingly, and answer every question, but under no circumstances does he wish his name to appear in print.

"Why not?" I ask.

"As a nation, we must live here in the underground."

"What does that mean?"

"There are unfavorable tendencies in Poland, and so we cannot allow ourselves the luxury of publicly acknowledging our Jewishness."

"But don't you teach Yiddish in the Jewish Social-Cultural Association? Isn't that acknowledging it?"

"My dear, the differences are subtle. We do not hide the fact that we are Jews, but neither do we flaunt it."

"Agreed, then. I will not print your name. But what about the rest?"

The man laughs. "That depends on the questions you ask."

"Where did you learn Yiddish?"

"At home in Lwów."

"Did you go to Jewish schools?"

"No, I graduated from the state school, but I grew up in the Jewish quarter. Nowhere in the world have I ever seen anything like our district in Lwów. Even in Israel the neighborhoods inhabited by the

Orthodox are, if I may say so, less Jewish. Until the age of twelve I was simply convinced that different religions and different nationalities were a minority in Poland."

"How did you discover that it is otherwise?"

"My father took me to the center of the city. There I saw an entirely different world, and I began asking him about it. Then he explained."

"Who was your father?"

"A carpenter. A very good craftsman. He made parquet floors. He inculcated in me the family tradition that one must live by the work of one's own hands; difficult, solid work. After graduation, father sent me to the railroad technical school. I never graduated, because the German-Soviet war broke out."

"Didn't you feel the true beginning of war in September, 1939?"

Written on the blackboard is the first word of the lesson: "Jew."

"In accordance with the Soviet-German pact,* Lwów fell in 1939 to the Soviet Union. I must admit that it meant very little to me."

"Poland lost its independence then."

"I agree, but we were Jews, and besides I was very young. I was sixteen and just experiencing my first great romance."

"What happened when the Germans entered the city?"

"I had traveled, completely by coincidence, deep into the Soviet Union. I was drafted into the Soviet army. I returned to Poland in October, 1945."

"Why didn't you stay in Lwów?"

"Because Lwów now belonged officially to the USSR."

"Earlier that had not bothered you."

"But later it did. After those several years' residence in the east, I very much wanted to return home. And it was not easy, although in the end I managed it."

"Why did you come specifically to Kraków?'

"Because my sister lived here. The rest of the family had died, but Poles had saved her. My sister was in the Lwów ghetto first. Then she crossed over to the Aryan side. The Siemaszkiewicz family hid her for fourteen months, along with two other Jews. They all survived."

"Is your sister still in Kraków?"

"No. In the mid-fifties someone insulted her while she was walking in the park with her children. He said something nasty about Jews. She returned home extremely indignant and decided then to leave. I did not want to part with her. I begged and pleaded but she would not yield.

*Soviet-German Pact—
The Ribbentrop-Molotov Pact of August 24, 1939.
The pact provided for friendship and aid between the two countries and contained a secret clause partitioning Poland.
In accordance with this provision, the Soviet army entered the territory of Poland on September 17, 1939.
The USSR occupied half of Poland.

She emigrated in 1956. They live in Israel."

"Why didn't you leave?"

"I had married a Pole. Such mixed marriages are not tolerated in Israel, unfortunately. My sons would have been discriminated against. I have a truly fine family. And so I did not want to expose them to that kind of shock."

"Do your sons know that you are a Jew?"

"Of course. They feel a great attachment to their father's origins. They demonstrate that through their great love and respect for me. And it is the same with my daughters-in-law, since both sons are married."

"How did you become a teacher of Yiddish?"

"A group of prospective students approached the JSCA. Since we no longer had a real teacher, we had to find a non-professional. There was a contest, and I turned out to know Yiddish best."

"That is what I cannot understand. After all, having a Polish family you do not use the language, do you?"

"That is why I was the best. Those who spoke Yiddish from time to time stopped speaking it well. They mix in Polish expressions, and they have lost the proper accent. I, on the other hand, locked the language of my childhood and youth inside me and carried it around in an untainted form all these years. And I must admit that I am very proud to be the person who possesses this treasure."

"Most of your students are Poles."

"There are no more young Jews in Kraków."

"But what do Poles want with Yiddish?"

"The Noble Prize obtained by Singer ennobled the language. And after all, it is in Poland, the former homeland of the Jews, that the great Yiddish literature arose. After the murder of the Jews it became herimetic because there was no one who could decipher it. This group of young people decided to master this language just in order to be able to read previously inaccessible works and enrich Polish culture with them. This is quite urgent, because the few remaining Jews here are growing old and will soon be dead."

"What are your students like?"

"Very fine indeed. Such enthusiasm for learning is rare. I always saw Poles as unfriendly toward Jews. During this teaching I have been able to see that it is otherwise. I have gotten to know my students very well, and I think that our meetings have become a good occasion for breaking down various barriers and suspicions. These result, often, from mere ignorance. I am glad that thanks to these lessons, Jewish culture has stopped being foreign to them."

"And what do these lessons give you?"

"An enormous amount. It's a fantastic feeling. Coming back, coming back at last... I lived so long without Jews, alone among Poles. I set a limit for myself, knowing that it is enough if my name and my physiognomy are accepted. And you know, from all those years I had only one single moment in the course of each day. In the mornings while I washed in the bathroom and shaved, I would talk to myself in Yiddish. I would look in the mirror and say, 'Oy, little Julius, Julek, but you're getting old. Not even your own mameh would recognize you anymore...'"

The best known of the Kraków Jews is Jonasz Stern, an outstanding painter, eccentric, and also famous for his striking good looks. He says of himself today, at the age of eighty-three, "The cat lets me live with him."

The tomcat is enormous, completely black, extremely lazy, and fully conscious of his privileges. He lies stretched out in the most unexpected places for hours. He never goes out, because Jonasz is afraid he might not return. The cat has no name. Stern calls him Son because, as he explains, "This is all the family I have."

They both live in a two-room apartment that serves simultaneously as a studio. Pictures fill all the free space. Among them there are the best-known works: the three-dimensional compositions using fish skeletons and animal bones. They all date from after the war. It is not difficult to decode the metaphors: death, destruction, disintegration. Stern comments with apparent calm, "A man who has lived through his own death could hardly tell the world anything else!"

Jonasz Stern was executed on July 20, 1943. It happened in the ravine at the end of Janowski Street, the site of mass executions for the Jews of the Lwów ghetto.

Three months earlier he had managed to escape from a transport to the Bełżec crematoria. He cut through the bars in the window of the cattle car, jumped from the train, and returned to the labor camp in Janów where Jews who not yet been murdered were confined. He returned there, since he had nowhere else to go. Most of the Poles he knew had been removed to camps in the depths of the USSR two years earlier, when the Russians occupied that region. Hiding Jews there was particularly difficult in 1943. There was danger not only from the Germans but also from the local Ukrainians. Jonasz could find no one who would run such a risk for a stranger.

Not long afterward, during the next action in the camp, he was picked up again. This time he was led, together with several score of people, straight to the ravine. They knew they were going to their death. Executions had been taking place at the ravine for many months. Jonasz cannot explain to me how it happened that a fraction of a second before the SS bullets hit the rows of people, he fell. Corpses covered him. He heard the screams and moans of the murdered. He fainted. When he came to, it was quiet. The Germans had left. Jonasz had neither the strength nor the courage to move. He lay there a long time, until the bodies around him became cold and stiff. Half-conscious, he remembered only that the corpses were always burned the next morning. During the night he extricated himself from the bodies. Smeared with the blood of strangers, caked on him from his hair to his feet, he ran into the depths of the forest.

A Polish railroad worker helped him. Jonasz hid with him for a week and then decided to make his way to Hungary, where the situation, in comparison to what was happening in Poland, was idyllic. Remaining in alliance with the German Reich, Hungary was still an independent and relatively liberal country. The Jews, although subjected to many discriminatory regulations, were not confined to ghettos. Official Polish refugee organizations were also active.

Jonasz traveled on foot through the Carpathians, the mountains of his youth. He could only move at night. This went on for many days. His only food was what the railroad man had given him: a loaf of bread, a half pound of sugar, and a bottle of valerian drops. He made it to the border half starved, badly beaten by Ukrainian shepherds he had encountered along the way. From then on, though, it was easier. From the Budapest Polish Committee he obtained documents in the name of Wiciński, clothing and money.

The Germans entered Hungary in March, 1944. They created ghettos for the Jews. Mass deportations to the death camps began. Jonasz managed to take shelter in a village where, after ten months the Russians arrived. He returned to Poland on the first transport. On April 29, 1945, he was again in Kraków. But the city was different, and Jonasz himself was no longer the same.

"Before that I had been a hooligan, a madman, always among people, always in the middle of the action. And afterward, well… I had a couple of friends, and most of all I loved being with nature. Holing up in the woods, kayaking, fishing, and painting, painting. Anything to avoid thinking about it, to forget, to muffle it."

Jonasz comes from Kałusz, a border city set in the foothills of the Carpathians. It was picturesque country, calm. Various nationalities lived there in harmony and, even though there were conflicts, there were never any pogroms. "Kałusz, my Kałusz," the old man repeats often during our conversation as he tells about the *tzaddik* who rode through the market square in a silver carriage; about the nearby cavern where Baal Shem Tov, the founder of Chassidism, lived as a hermit for several years before setting out into the world; about the fairs to which Jewish merchants traveled from distant parts. "I always thought, even when I grew up, that Kałusz was a big glorious city. But I went there after the war and saw it—oh, how small and poor. They had made a park in the market square with a golden Lenin standing in the middle, and I could find no graves in our cemetery, only a monument with a red star."

Jonasz moved from Kałusz to Kraków at the age of twenty. He wanted to study and become a painter. He was already a communist. He had a pair of strikes that he had organized in his hometown, a short stay in prison, and a heated argument with his family behind him. His father and mother could not get over the fact that Jonasz had departed from religion and, what is more, demonstrated it with defiant nonchalance. On the High Holy Days he would stroll in front of the synagogue, munching with relish on a large piece of sausage; afterward he often got into fights with devout youngsters who, outraged and insulted, threw themselves upon him in wild fury.

In Kraków, Jonasz began the artist's life in the bohemian style of those days. The milieu was extensive and varied. The exponents of abstract art were in the ascendancy, but realists painting classic genre pieces, portraits, and landscapes had the clientele. Jonasz enrolled in the Fine Arts Academy and took lodgings with a poor Jewish widow. They lived together in one dark room: the landlady, her daughter and two sons, and five students of painting and sculpture. The young men formed a commune. They had common funds, although they were usually bankrupt because even though they took whatever work was available, they made so little that they often could not pay the rent. Then their landlady would extend credit. They spent most days in town. Evenings they held court in the kitchen, cooking, drinking vodka, and to keep their hands in, sketching each other. At night they laid mattresses on the floor and slept in a row. Jonasz lived that way for six years.

When he remembers those times, his face still brightens. Kraków was bubbling over. Dozens of cabarets, literary cafes, and clubs were active. Life had a good rhythm. Mad, drunken nights, violent romances, discussions about art fierce enough to end the closest friendships, brawls with anti-Semitic fraternities at the university. Jonasz felt wonderful.

He also took shape as an artist. He became an abstract painter with a personal, expressive style. Together with his friends, he founded the famous Kraków Group, whose members proclaimed a revolution not only in art, but also in society. For this, Jonasz spent half a year in Bereza Kartuska.*

When the war broke out, he and his wife escaped to the Soviet zone of occupation. They settled in Lwów, where Jonasz became the president of a painters' cooperative. The Germans found them there. Both went to the ghetto. His wife died in Auschwitz. She committed suicide by throwing herself onto the electrified fence.

Back in Kraków after the war, Jonasz began modestly. He decorated shop windows. In those days, nevertheless, people often told him, 'With a biography like yours you should become an important artist.' He did not want to become one, because he did not want to paint in the new style imported from the Soviet Union. Socialist realism was universally obligatory then, without exception. The minister of culture told Jonasz, who was one of the few still producing abstract paintings, "You are no communist. You are an agent of American imperialism."

*Bereza Kartuska—The prison in which the Polish authorities confined troublesome political opponents during the second half of the 1930s.

Jonasz only joined the Academy of Fine Arts after the death of Stalin. He began as vice rector. Freedom again prevailed in art. Jonasz slowly acquired further academic titles. He has been a full professor for twenty years. His official career ended in 1968, however, when the Party secretary came to him then and said with sudden solicitude, "Comrade, you are very tired and overworked now. You have no time for your own work." "Say no more," Jonasz interrupted. From the first of the next month he ceased fulfilling all his functions and became an ordinary lecturer. Six years later he retired.

In the forty years since the war, Jonasz Stern has accomplished everything an artist could desire. He has earned fame and recognition. He has been able to devote himself to his art, transfer it to others, and teach younger generations. He has had scores of exhibitions in Poland and other parts of the world. He has won many competitions and earned a multitude of prizes. He has been honored with the highest distinctions.

Today he sits before me on a narrow bed, frail, bent, with a sleeping cat on his knees. We look at photographs: Jonasz with men friends, with women, walking through fields, with a fishing rod, in a kayak. Looking at one of the portraits I cannot help saying, "Mr. Stern, what a beautiful man you were!"

The old man takes the picture from me. He looks at it for a long time, without smiling. Then he lays it aside, face down. For a moment we are both silent.

Then I ask, "Are you still painting?"

"Of course," Stern answers. "I am unable not to work. There is no alternative. To stop working, for me, means to stop living." Jonasz smiles

Jonasz Stern, alone in his apartment-stud
with his beloved cat, whom he calls "Sor

with mild resignation. "But I have less and less strength, less and less..."

The cat wakes up and yawns widely.

"What, Son?" Jonasz says and strokes him delicately. "You know how much I like you."

The cat stretches, jumps from his knees, and walks slowly out of the room. Jonasz watches him, and then turns to me.

"You know, I have this dream. I found a photograph with a view of Kałusz, and I want to do one more picture in my life. I will paint it realistically. It will be like this..." Jonasz sketches it in the air with his upraised hands. "Kałusz, and above it hangs a *tallis*, drooping."

Roman Spira is descended in a direct line from the famous Krakow cabbalist, *gaon*, and rector of the Talmudic faculty Natan Nat Spira, who died in 1633.

The Spira family has lived in Krakow ever since. Until the end of the nineteenth century, it cultivated the tradition of its great ancestor. They lived according to the rules of the Law in exemplary piety, and all the male members of the line obtained extensive religious educations. Roman's father, a merchant himself, graduated from the Higher Talmudic School in his youth. Of his three sons, however, who were born at the beginning of the new century, each chose a different path.

The oldest, a former *legionista*,* assimilated to Polishness and lived in Polish surroundings. The youngest, a doctor of philosophy, studied in Vienna for years at the school of the famous rabbi Zwi Perez Chajes and remained almost exclusively among Jews. Roman, however, found himself in the middle not only in regards to age but also to his choice. He graduated from *cheder* and later a Polish *gimnazium* and the Commercial School, worked in his father's shop, was married beneath the *chuppah*, and yet visited the synagogue only once a year, for *Yom Kippur*, and made friends with Jews and Poles alike.

More than half a century had to pass before Roman Spira, old and lonely after the death of his wife, returned to his roots. He has dedicated the last ten years to studying the history of Kraków's Jews. Today, at eighty-three, he is the author of two books: a guide to the Remu Cemetery and a biography of eminent Kraków rabbis.

From the end of the fifteenth century, an extraordinarily intensive

*Legionista—Soldier of the Polish Legions commanded by Jozef Piludski, which fought during the First World War. This unit had great respect in inter-war Poland as one of those which helped in the recovery of independence after 123 years of subjugation.

intellectual life developed in Kazimierz; as a result Kraków became a center of Judaistic religious learning for all of Europe. In the seventeenth century it was even asserted that "never has there been such learning among the dispersed sons of Israel as there is in Poland," and the Jewish City of Kazimierz was called the holy community on the Rivers Vistula and Wilga.

Great rabbis, teachers, and Jewish spiritual leaders lived and worked here during the course of those two hundred years, such as Jakub Polak, the founder of the first academy in Kazimierz, who in recognition of his great learning in Hebrew literature and Holy Scripture was named chief rabbi of the Polish Jews by the king; famous mystics, confessors, and propogators of the practical *Cabbala*, such as Jezajasz Horowic and Natan Nat Spira. And above all Mojżesz Isserles, Remu, venerated to this day as a great man of wisdom by Jews around the world. In his work known as *The Map*, he adapted the preeminent work of talmudism, the *Szulchan Aruch* of Joseph Karo, to the needs of Ashkenazi Jews. To this day those two books, published together, constitute a codex and casebook in Jewish civil and religious law. Remu also took up philosophy, geometry, and astronomy. His tombstone is engraved:

"From Moses / the prophet / to Moses / Maimonides / there never arose another like Moses / Isserles."

It is to them that Roman Spira dedicated his work. Writing it was preceded not only by years of arduous research but also by years of intensive study, because, as Spira says, he "turned out to be very undereducated." And he adds, "But fortunately, it is possible to learn even in one's seventies."

Preserving the oldest Jewish cemetery in Poland, the famous Remu Cemetery, which belongs to the synagogue of the same name, became Roman's second passion. The Remu cemetery was founded in 1551, and since the end of the seventeenth century there have been no further burials in it. In the two hundred years leading up to the Second World War, there were only forty-seven graves there. They were held in great respect.

During the war the gravestones served the Germans as targets for shooting practice and were smashed to small pieces by the bullets. Only one *matzevah* came through intact—that of Mojżesz Isserles. Legend had proclaimed that a curse would fall on anyone who desecrated the famous rabbi's grave and the profaner would die within the year. Even the SS feared this threat. Remu's grave survived and is to this day a place of pilgrimage for Chassidim from all over the world. For many years after the war, however, it stood in a completely empty cemetery, since the rest of the destroyed *matzevahs* had been used to build a "wailing wall."

Only in 1958, thanks to the efforts of the head of the congregation, Meir Jakubowicz, were Joint funds used to conduct excavations in the cemetery. The results surpassed the most optimistic expectations: seven hundred graves were unearthed, which had probably been covered during the Swedish invasion in the seventeenth century. Together they constitute a monument of funerary art, and many possess unique artistic value. The oldest are more than 430 years old.

This was a great architectural revelation. But it led no further. The headstones were set up in the cemetery, and there it ended.

Roman Spira, 82, by his famous ancestor's grave in the Remu cemetery.

There was a lack both of money for their conservation and of people with a knowledge of Hebrew who could decode the epitaphs and make a record of the gravestones. But they could become priceless material for the study of the Krakow community.

The only attempt at a systematic description of the newly discovered *matzevah* has been undertaken by an amateur, Roman Spira. For five years he worked in the cemetery on his own, at his own expense, but without the requisite preparation. He copied gravestone inscriptions and sketched the ornaments. Surrounded by dictionaries, he tried to decipher the texts. This was work for a thoroughgoing Hebraist, since abbreviations specific to given times and styles were used in the epitaphs. For someone with only an average knowledge of Hebrew, on the other hand, penetrating the crabbed texts became an enormous and often fruitless task.

Spira managed to translate only a few of the epitaphs, including the one found on the grave of his famous greatgrandfather Natan. Yet he made out all seven hundred names and the accompanying dates of birth and death. For a nonprofessional, this was a great success. Another contribution by Spira was the copying of the texts. At present, after almost thirty years of the action of rain, frost, and the poisoned atmosphere, many inscriptions have already disappeared.

"The *matzevahs* are decaying, falling apart," Spira worries. "They must be saved immediately, because otherwise they will be irrevocably destroyed. I know, however, that this is unrealistic because of the lack of people and means. I fear, therefore, that my book will soon become a document of the past." Besides precise locations of gravestones and transcriptions of those he managed to read, Spira's guide to the Remu

Cemetery also includes many pictures of particular *matzevahs* and faithful drawings of the ornaments. All of it, enclosed in a large portfolio, is waiting for a publisher— without results so far.

"It's my fault to a great degree," Roman Spira explains. "I haven't advertised my book and haven't gone around to the publishers, because it is truly enough for me that I have prepared it."

"Isn't that an excess of modesty?" I ask. "After all, these books, and particularly the guide to Remu would be very useful."

Spira smiles. "No, this is not the result of too much modesty, but of age. But of course I believe that they will be printed someday. They will be one more memento that remains after us, the last Jews of Kraków. For me, however, their main significance is as a private reckoning with myself. Because these books are—how to put it—a certain propitiation, a paying of a debt."

"A debt? To whom?"

"You know, before the war I strongly disliked the *chałaciarz.** I was ashamed of them. They made me nervous because they stood out, and I thought they would lead to anti-Semitism. And at the same time I was not upset by a priest's cassock or by a nun in a big veil—only by the *chalat* and sidecurls. Only after the war did I realize how stupid I had been. I understood that it was exactly thanks to them, those Orthodox and Chassidim, thanks to the great rabbis, that Judaism survived. They created it and passed it on; not us, the intelligentsia who followed the *Haskalah.* I understood as well that you can be a Pole, a patriot, because you live on this land, but above all you have to be a Jew."

**chałaciarz*—Popular prewar term for Jews who dressed traditionally, in *pais* (sidecurls) and *yarmulka* (cap).

There are more than 430 Jewish cemeteries in Poland. Most are a no-man's land. Abandoned by everyone, they are falling into ruin.

CHAPTER SIX

THE SEEDLING

Bar Mitzvah is one of the most important days in the life of a Jew. The boy becomes a man. Summoned to public prayer for the first time, he will count from then on among the *minyan*. Entry into the circle of prayer is a symbolic entry into the Jewish community.

Bar Mitzvah is a joyous holiday all over the world; in Warsaw on May 18, 1985, however, the joy was exceptional. For the first time in thirty years a thirteen-year-old boy stood on the *bimah* in the center of the synagogue. He did not stand among his contemporaries but among old men separated from him by at least two generations—two absent generations.

All the old men had assembled for this: the sick ones, even the ones who rarely come to pray. They crowded tightly around the *bimah*, on which the small thin boy wearing an abundant *tallis* was singing the prayers in a none-too-certain voice. "That's the seedling," one of them has told me earlier, "who has grown from a sea of nothing. He has grown from fallow ground that we long believed absolutely barren."

That day, however, the synagogue was full. All the benches were taken, and an old woman who arrived somewhat late had to ask me to move over and make room for her. She asked me in German, but I knew her by sight and answered in Polish. She did a double take. "Aren't you from an excursion?"

It was my turn to be surprised. "From an excursion? Why?"

"Because there are so many people here today," she said. "So many young people and it's usually completely empty. I thought a tour from America had come."

When I explained that it was a *Bar Mitzvah*, the woman did not want to believe me at first. Then she fell silent for a long while, and finally said quietly, "Thank you, God, for letting me live through such a moment."

Bergson House, situated on the right bank in Warsaw, once belonged to the Jewish community. A plaque set into the front wall even recalls this fact. The building is enormous. Before the war it contained a dormitory and a school for Jewish youth. The man who paid for it equipped it fully with the latest in everything young people could need, including an auditorium. After the war the dormitory was turned into housing for surviving Jews whose children were taught in the school, and Ida Kaminska's theater gave guest performances in the auditorium. Later the Jews left, the school was used as a "normal" kindergarten, and the part of the building containing the auditorium was transferred to a puppet theater. The plaque remained, along with one last Jewish family. Or, rather, Jewish-Polish.

Apartment number 1 on the second floor is strange, somewhat neglected, but full of charm. It suggests a labyrinth. Many rooms in a small space: alcoves of a sort, stairs, entresols. And in them a multitude of original and amusing objects, theatrical decorations, pictures, above all, books. They fill the walls, and shelves hang even on the doors. Among the books are unusually valuable old editions: sixteenth- and seventeenth-century Bibles and Hebrew prayer books.

The four of them live here: Ninel Kameraz, her husband Bogdan Kos, and their two sons, fifteen-year-old Łukasz and Mateusz, the one who had the *Bar Mitzvah*—the Seedling.

Ninel looks young. I am astonished when she says she is forty-eight. "That's right," she confirms. "Forty-eight, and enough experience for twice that old. Because when I think how many strikes I have against me," she says, counting them off on her fingers, "to be a Jew, and a poor Jew at that, and furthermore from a communist family. That's a tough potion to swallow. Well, and then there's my name." She spells it out: "N-I-N-E-L. Lenin backwards! A true mark of Cain."

"And was it always so obvious?"

"And how! You yourself admit that it's a rarity. One would pass the word on to another. They all knew. After all, you knew it, too."

"That's true. Did they tease you a lot?"

"Oy! I was always glad that I wasn't immortal."

"How did you get such a name?"

"They were fashionable among communists. My sister, who's eight years older, is named Rema after the first letters of a slogan that was very popular in the Soviet Union in the twenties—Revolution, Electrification, *Mir* [peace]"

"No!"

"They used to think up such miracles, and afterward it was hard for their children to live with them."

"Tell me about your parents."

"They both came from poverty. He came from a small town. She came from Wilno. They both grew up in families where there were a lot of children and there was very little money, and so they were sort of naturally drawn towards communism. It was a chance."

"But their parents were religious."

"Of course. As a young boy, Papa's father drew a ticket for a twenty-five year pull in the Czarist army. He escaped from that and got some papers from a Lithuanian named Kamerazas. He shortened the name and it stayed that way. But aside from that they were a typical Jewish family: devout, traditional, and poor. Grandfather was a carter without a horse. He only bought one later when he sold Papa."

"What does that mean?"

"It's a strange story. My father had severe epilepsy. That might be why his mother loved him the most of all her children. When she was dying, she called for him, but by the time he got to the hospital, she was already gone. Daddy wanted to see her, so an orderly took him downstairs to the morgue. He opened some sort of cabinet or box there, but he opened the wrong one. There was nothing in it but amputated legs and arms. Papa—he was in his teens then and a tailor's apprentice—went home and immediately fell asleep. He slept through the funeral and the next day and the day after. Finally they called a doctor from the city, who offered to buy the patient as a guinea pig. Grandfather agreed, because Papa would have died at home. He had to be fed somehow, and that was before intravenous was known. The doctor took the sleeper, and Grandfather bought a horse with the money. Papa slept twenty-three days and came to, in the sense of recovering his awareness over a period of many months. That doctor took him all around Poland and displayed him during lectures. For Europe it was an exceptionally rare case of sleeping sickness. The doctor described him in a book as 'the sickness of patient K.' Forty years later I found that account in a medical textbook."

"I understand that your father returned to normal."

"Oh, yes. He was even particularly gifted. Later, when he was in Moscow with Mama, he was selected to be one of the so-called red professors. That was a kind of school for geniuses. The Party was preparing academic cadre at a stepped-up tempo. There were several dozen gifted students, and most of them had had only a few months of schooling. They worked very hard, twelve or fourteen hours a day. First they finished their studies, then they had various seminars, and then they wrote their theses and became professors. The whole thing lasted four or five years. Afterward Papa became head of the philosophy department. Marxist-Leninist, of course, because that's all there was. At the same time he enrolled as an auditor in medical school. He had always wanted to be a doctor, but the Party wouldn't let him. He also got an apartment in Moscow, near the Kremlin. Two rooms for him, Mama, and Rema. That was incredible luxury. In those days the average in Moscow was eight people per room. Papa immediately wrote to his father that he had become a professor. Grandfather carried the letter to the prayer house, and to them, simple Jews from a little Polish town, it was entirely obvious that a professor was some sort of better doctor. From that time on letters arrived in Moscow with descriptions of the illnesses of the whole community. Papa, who did not want to disappoint his father, went to doctors and found out and wrote back how they were to be treated."

"And your mother? What did she do?"

"Mama was a very ambitious person. In this period she was going to the conservatory. She wanted to be a conductor. But the idyll ended quickly. After a year Papa was arrested. On the exact day I was born. That was a horrible time: 1937. Nobody believed anybody, and everybody was informing. Papa had brought his brothers and sisters to Moscow earlier. Now they locked them all up. Uncle Abram was in the camps for eighteen years and Aunt Rachela just as long. Once I calculated that our close relatives did sixty-four years between them. Mama was left, thanks to which we didn't become orphans. We were brought up at home. That became a nightmare, too. Mama was kicked out of the conservatory. She couldn't find work. She became very ill and went blind in one eye. Additional tenants were assigned to our apartment. All we had was the smaller room. Then the war broke out. Mama worked around the clock in munitions factories. In general, we didn't see her. Rema suffered the worst. She was a teenager then and she had to take care of the home and me. There was a terrible hunger. Fortunately, I don't remember much of that."

"When did your father return?"

"After nine years, in 1946. The Union of Polish Patriots* was active then, pulling former communists out of the camps. There weren't many left, because the majority had been shot at the end of the thirties. Papa survived because he had epileptic seizures during the interrogations. That bored them, and they sent him to the far north. When he was

*Union of Polish Patriots—Organization of Polish communists created by Stalin after the breaking of diplomatic relations between the wartime Polish government in exile and the USSR. The Union of Polish Patriots became the germ of future communist authorities dependent on the USSR.

released he received permission to travel through Moscow, but only for twenty-four hours. He was on his way to Poland. I was just coming home from school with Mama. The concierge greeted us, saying, 'Your husband has returned.' Mama was struck dumb, but I started shouting 'Papa! Papa at last!' The official version for the children had been that Daddy was in a sanatorium. So I waited constantly for him and imagined how beautiful and elegant and young he was. Unconscious with joy, I ran upstairs and burst into the room, and there at the table sat an old man dressed in horrible rags. On his skull there was sparse gray hair, he didn't have a tooth in his head, he was dirty and his face was a strange grayish-green. 'That's not my papa!' I shrieked and started to cry. He put out his hand to me and said 'Daughter.' Then I ran away and hid outdoors. That was my first meeting with my father."

"Did it get better?"

"After a year of working at it we managed to travel to see him in Warsaw, and then we made friends quickly. And you know, we truly came to love each other. But I still have something on my conscience."

"Everybody has."

"I studied acoustical engineering at the Warsaw Polytechnic, and in my third year I transferred to Wrocław. We had friends there. They were Papa's acquaintances—he was a Jew, she was a Pole who couldn't stand Jews, outside of a few exceptions. Once Papa decided to visit me. And I have to remark that he had an extraordinarily Semitic appearance. Additionally he was very short and spoke terrible Polish. That woman told me, 'You'd better not take your father to your dormitory.' Daddy came, we stayed with them, and in the afternoon we went out for a walk. I can remember every detail. We walked near the dormitory and I even pointed out my window to him, but I didn't invite him in. And yet that was my home, even if I did share it with the other girls. Papa was very delicate. He said nothing and never mentioned it afterward but it remained with me all those years like a great stain."

"Does that mean that you were ashamed of your Jewishness in general?"

"That's complicated. In Moscow our language was Russian and you didn't talk about the rest. After we arrived in Poland, on the contrary, Jewishness was, if I can put it that way, all-encompassing. My parents spoke Yiddish to each other, we lived in a house where we were among no one but Jews, and that was a big colony of several hundred people. I went to a Jewish school. I even have report cards with the grades written in Yiddish. At home there were Jewish newspapers and books, and all my parent's friends were Jews, too. What more could there be?"

"How did all that make you feel?"

"On the one hand, normal. That was my place. But on the other hand, I felt the weight of humps on my back: Jewishness, poverty, communism."

"After all they had lived through, did your parents remain communists?"

"They went on believing that the system is good, that there had only been mistakes by the NKVD, Beria. At the end of the forties Mama was still saying that Stalin was a man of wisdom and a great leader, that he didn't know what they were doing. And I can understand that. She was defending herself. After all, nobody can reveal herself to be such an imbecile in her own eyes."

"The thing I don't understand is your poverty. After the war, communists—those good prewar comrades—usually had great careers."

"When my father returned to Poland, he was offered a splendid post … in the Ministry of Internal Affairs. He turned it down, and there were no more attractive offers. So he became an office worker in a cooperative and remained there on a very modest salary until he retired."

"Didn't he feel that he'd missed the boat?"

"Yes, he felt very down and out and deeply hurt. They had both been brave enough to put a lot of distance between themselves and their parents, and what they ended up with was regrettable and artificial. I'm not talking for one minute about their careers or about communism but about their whole lives. They had very little that was good, and they didn't have it for long, and afterward they had a nightmare. It was difficult for them in Poland, too. They always felt foreign, and they were never assimilated."

"Did they want to be assimilated?"

"They might not even have wanted to be, but they spoke well of Poles. Being Polish was something good and successful."

"Would they have been able to assimilate?"

"No. Even for me it took long years. To assimilate in Poland is very difficult."

"Why?"

"Now I don't know anymore, because I'm on this side, but I remember that there were such walls: religion, anti-Semitism. Not so much unpleasantness as just an enormous wall."

"Did you often encounter anti-Semitic behavior?"

"Oh, petty anti-Semitism was my daily bread. How many times I rode with Papa in the streetcar and heard remarks around us about Jews, that they are this and that ... and those regrets that they weren't all poisoned, they they weren't all asphyxiated, that Hitler didn't finish his job. And that's the answer to your question about the internal acceptance of my Jewishness. It was hard for me to accept because others didn't accept it in me or above all in my parents. For a child, the most important thing is for her parents to be respected so that she can admire them herself. With us it was the other way around. And besides, at home I heard terrifying tales about who had survived what and how exhausted they were. Papa, Mama, relatives, acquaintances. Papa even competed with Henryk, my sister's husband. Henryk was in the Warsaw ghetto, and later, on Aryan papers, he ended up in Mathausen camp. He wasn't circumcised, and so he lasted there until the end of the war. Those two could argue for hours about where it was worse—in a German camp or in a Soviet camp. And it went on that way for years. They couldn't break out of the vicious circle. And I wanted a normal life!"

"Did you get one?"

"If such a thing is ever possible, yes. Thanks to Bogdan, above all. Every time I met a new boy I felt that I ought to bring it up honestly and say, 'I am a Jew.' When I admitted it to Bogdan for the fourth time he said gently, 'I know, Ninel. You've already told me.' And that was the end of the discussion. Bogdan was the first person who did not have a preconceived opinion on the subject of Jews. He didn't accuse them, but he didn't fall down on his knees in front of them. You know, to me philo-Semitism, which is a love of Jews, is just as suspect as anti-Semitism, with its almost physiological hatred. And besides his matter-of-fact approach, Bogdan also knew a lot about Judaism, about Jewish culture. A lot more than I did. He also knew a little Yiddish and when he visited my parents he would take along the *Folks-Styme* newspaper and read to Papa. Papa adored that."

"Didn't he want his second son-in-law to be Jewish, too?"

"He wanted a Jew, of course, but since there weren't any Jews... and Mama always told me, 'Bogdan is from such a good Polish home.' She was even proud of that."

"What happened to your sister's family?"

"They left in 1968. I told you about Henryk, Rema's husband. He survived on Aryan papers. After his return from Mathausen to Warsaw, he wanted to go back to his own surname, Braun. In the city council they told him, of course, that's possible. All he needed was two people to testify that Braun was his real name. But in the whole city he couldn't find two witnesses. Nobody had survived, and Henryk had to continue using the name Goliszewski. And afterward, in 1968, a meeting was called in his office and he was reminded that his real name was Braun. So they took their three children and emigrated to Australia.

"Papa also had an adventure in those days with his first name. He was called to an office and asked 'Mr. Chaskiel Kameraz?' 'Yes.' 'Do you intend to emigrate?' 'No.' 'Are you aware of the Polish specifics?' 'I don't really see what you're getting at,' Papa said in surprise. And they went on: 'Don't you want to change your first name?' Papa replied, 'Now I understand those specifics.' 'So will you change it?' Papa didn't say anything for a moment, and then he stated, 'My father gave me the name Chaskiel. I would willingly change it. But you understand that first I must ask permission.' They nodded and Papa went on, 'The only problem is that he died thirty years ago.' And so they left him in peace."

"Your father stayed in Poland?"

"He was very ill and could not leave. I stayed as well. Bogdan and I moved in here so that we could take care of him. My mother had already died."

"By then there weren't many Jews left."

"I have survived many departures. A lot of Jews left in 1948 and 1949. Later in 1956, thousands passed through Warsaw en route from the Soviet Union to Israel. Among them was my father's sister Rachela. It is difficult to describe that kind of misery. What got to me most of all, though, was the emigration of 1968. Then people who had already put down roots were leaving. And when they left, I felt an emptiness for the first time."

"Do you ever regret having stayed?"

"No. I had grown up in Poland. I have a familiar environment here, friends."

"And your Jewishness?"

"That became my private, absolutely personal affair. It was that way until the birth of my children, or rather until the moment when they grew somewhat. When the boys were four, five years old, I took them to the Jewish cemetery, to their grandparents' graves. I told them that I am a Jew and they are Jews after me. That was what you might call the elementary level. The rest was worse. I thought I should teach them something, but I really didn't know what. And here Bogdan was a great help. He told the boys about the Bible, the *Talmud*, about the history of the Jews, and above all about the Judeo-Greco culture, which he feels is the basis for Western Civilization. He showed them their roots. That theme was always present in our home. Later, in 1983, when we were in the synagogue, one of the people who was praying came up to us. He asked if our sons wanted to learn Hebrew. Mateusz at once reacted with enthusiasm, and Łukasz also agreed. That was when he called in Mr. Szapiro. We met, and the boys started going to him for lessons. Łukasz soon wanted to quit going. I told him, though, that he had to learn for a year. Afterward he could decide, when he knew what it was about. And so it was. He came to me and said, 'Mama, I know I'm a Jew but I don't like it.' I didn't coax him anymore."

"With Mateusz it was completely different."

"That's right. He found something there that was his and was true. He wanted to continue, and when Mr. Szapiro suggested the *Bar Mitzvah*, he agreed with joy."

"Of two brothers raised the same way and almost the same age, one chose Polishness and the second chose Jewishness."

"We wonder about that ourselves. Of course there's no clear-cut answer. Łukasz is more tied to—even fascinated by—Polish culture. He knows a lot, he reads, he watches. He writes stories and plays for children himself, and he does it really well. Mateusz, on the other hand, had a metaphysical, religious inclination since childhood. I remember how when he was little and barely knew how to walk he was already asking about death. How is it possible? What happens afterward? And he wasn't looking for a biological explanation. The intention of the question was apparent. And one more thing. More than a year ago a boy came to Warsaw—Peter—and lived with us a while. He was a Polish Jew who had gone to Israel. He served in the army there, became religious, and he came here—for exactly what reasons, nobody knows. A little bit crazy, a bit of a fanatic. He got along with Mateusz, but not with Łukasz, no. The boys were studying Hebrew then and Peter gave Mateusz a *tallis, tallis katon* and *tefilin*. I think that all of it together had an influence on the boy's decision."

"Your son is more and more religious. What about you? I asked Bogdan. He said that if he called himself a religious man it would be heresy."

"As usual, he's too modest. I am convinced that when he dies he will sit at the table with the Lord God."

"And then there's you, Ninel."

"I have a deep feeling that everything is in order. I am a Jew and my ancestors arranged that with God. It has lasted a long time and it has been difficult—it is not easy to be the people chosen by Him. But it happened. Of course, I would rather my links with Him were more tangible, that I had been brought up in the religion. But it was otherwise. Too bad. Yet in the end that is external. No, I have no doubts in this matter. And no fears."

Mateusz Kos is shown in the tefi
put on during morning pray

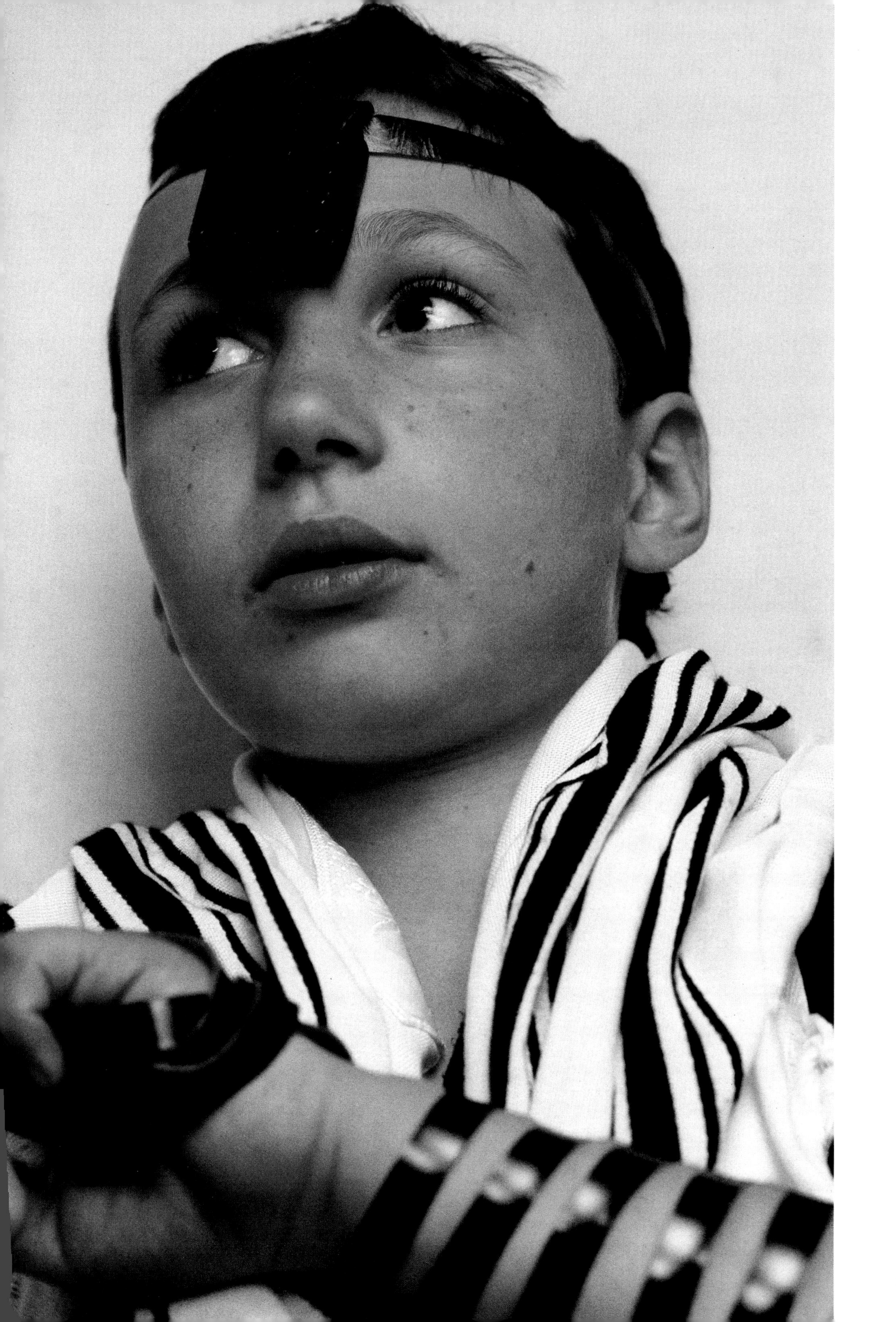

Ninel Kameraz-Kos in her apartment.

Next page: Mateusz Kos in the home of his teacher, Mojżesz Szapiro, during a religious lesson.

Underwo

"What does it mean to you to be a Jew?"

Mateusz bows his head and does not speak for a long moment. Then he begins, with a slight stutter. "It's hard for me to say ... I never thought about it. To me it's, well ... normal. When I was little, Mama told me that I am a Jew but Daddy isn't and that the tribe is inherited from the father and the nation from the mother. Later I went to church, to catechism, with my friends from school, but it bored me so I stopped

going. Then I asked Mama if Jews have holidays, too, and if we could observe them. Catholics have theirs, and I wanted to have something too."

"Did you start observing them?"

"Yes. *Pesach* and *Purim.* It was certainly not all in accordance with the rules. Daddy cued us. I also read a thick book, *The History of Israel.* I took notes and later I recited the history of Esther. Also I always make raisin wine for *Purim.* And Łukasz led the *seder.* I asked, and he answered. We also went to synagogue, but we couldn't tell up from down. Only when I started studying with Mr. Szapiro did it become clear."

Mateusz during prayers in his apartment.

"Was learning Hebrew difficult?"

"The alphabet, yes, but after that it wasn't hard at all. Easier than a lot of things in mathematics."

"Did Mr. Szapiro also tell you about the traditions and history of the Jews?"

"Not much. He is very kind to me and cares about me but he thinks that I am a little child. Like, for instance, when there was the Hebrew word for "seed," Mr. Szapiro explained to me that plants grow from seeds. Or that a bird is a kind of animal with wings. And that's a hassle."

"Yet you had a *Bar Mitzvah*."

"Well, right. I remind him of that myself. After all, I'm really an adult now."

"Tell me about the *Bar Mitzvah*."

"From the beginning of our lessons Mr. Szapiro talked to me about it. Lukasz refused; I agreed. They wanted to do it right after my thirteenth birthday in accordance with the rules. But I thought I didn't know enough, so I was almost four months late. I studied a lot."

"On the Thursday before the *Bar Mitzvah*, when you had your examination, you fainted in the synagogue."

"Wednesday evening I sat up a long time over the Torah. On Thursday I overslept, and I still had to run to the store to do the shopping. There was a long line, so I didn't manage to eat breakfast. At ten I was already at the synagogue with Mama. Only the *minyan* was there. I stood a long time near the *bimah*. I waited and waited. I was

e Kameraz-Kos family.

terribly frightened, and then suddenly I felt that I couldn't do it. I started to cry and to say something to Mr. Szapiro, but he wasn't listening. Then I fell. The floor there is stone. I was in pain and I don't remember anything. I woke up on a bench. I was lying there and they were standing over me and each one was offering me his heart medicine. They are always carrying nitroglycerin. Well, it ended with them rubbing cologne water on my temples, and I quickly said all the prayers. Afterward they took me home."

"On Saturday it went better."

"I wasn't so nervous anymore. It was a different atmosphere— a full synagogue, my friends. Once I stepped onto the *bimah*, it became totally quiet. Behind my back I could feel that they were all listening. It was even sort of amusing, because as soon as I started reading, all these old gentlemen began prompting me. Every one of them! But completely unnecessarily, because I knew it well."

"You invited a lot of people to the *Bar Mitzvah*."

"Not so they would praise me, word of honor. I wanted them to see, because after all it was my holiday. The most important birthday in my life."

"But the ones who were most moved, aside from your parents, were those old religious Jews."

"Oh, yes. That was very nice. When I walked off the *bimah*, they all hugged and kissed me even though I didn't know a lot of them. And Mr. Szapiro and Mr. Boguchwal cried."

"You know that in fact there are few Jews in Poland. There

certainly are no young ones your age. Don't you feel slightly isolated among those old people? Aren't you sorry that you are one of the last?"

"It's a great pity to me that there are so few Jews and that they are so old. And it's sad that there might not be any more.... Sometimes I think, What will it be like when I'm old, when I'm forty?"

"And how do your schoolmates react to your being Jewish?"

"When we quarrel, some of them shout 'Jew, Judas.' And I shout back, 'You Pole, you." Except that they think 'Jew' is offensive and 'Pole' isn't. But it doesn't bother me."

"And your teachers?"

"The teachers treat me absolutely normally."

"How do you get along with your brother? Doesn't it bother you that one of you wants above all to be a Pole and the other one above all a Jew?"

"I don't see anything bad about that. It all comes down to choice."

"Do you talk about it?"

"A little. He doesn't want to depend upon a religion. He says he wants to be free."

"And you?"

"My religion does not hinder me in any way."

"Don't you treat it a little bit like an adventure, like a big game of 'playing Jew'?"

"It was fun—and even more than that—especially at the holidays. Afterward, that changed. The border between fun and not-fun was Hebrew. Because it's so much work, right? And praying, the *Bar Mitzvah*, that's a totally serious matter. After all, if I hadn't taken it so seriously I wouldn't have fainted."

"For thousands of years being a Jew has involved persecution, suffering, even death. Do you realize that this is a serious decision and that even if it's good and nice that's only for now, and in somewhat altered circumstances you could suffer?"

"Yes, I know something about that. Now Mr. Szapiro has suggested circumcision to me. In Poland there is no *mohel*, so the Jewish community will organize it abroad somewhere, in Vienna or Amsterdam. When they proposed that to me, I thought that sometime in the future it could be dangerous. But I've made up my mind. I've had the *Bar Mitzvah* and I need the rest."

"How do you understand the *Bar Mitzvah*? What does it oblige you to do?"

"Not to renounce it."

"Not to renounce what?"

"Jewishness."

"So now how would you answer the question, What does it mean to be a Jew?"

"The way I see it, it seems simple at first. And then the more you know, the harder and harder it becomes, being a Jew. Especially in Poland."

"But I see that you're not turning back."

"No. I'll take the risks."

CHAPTER SEVEN

NO FEAR IN ME

Szymon Datner, Ph.D., associate professor of history, eminent Hebraist, is a member of the Presidium of the Congregation of the Mosaic Faith, vice president of the Jewish Historical Institute, and the author of fifteen books and more than 150 articles dealing principally with German crimes in Poland and the martyrdom of the Jewish nation.

"Our conversation will conclude a book about today's Polish Jews. Before I begin asking questions, of which I have prepared a great many, I would like to ask you to tell me about your life. You are far more than an outstanding academic and a great moral authority in Poland and in Jewish circles around the world. You are also a man with a very interesting biography."

"You have mentioned the book, so I would like to begin by saying something on that subject. I am an old man, I am not in the best of health, I have a great deal of work and limited time in which to finish it. So I am not generous in sharing that time. But since what you—you and your husband—are doing is very close to my heart, I am at your disposal without limitation."

"Thank you."

"And write what I have said."

"If you wish."

"I request it."

"Now let me ask you to tell me about yourself."

"I was born in Kraków in 1902. The beginnings of my life were very ordinary. My father was a silk dealer and had a small shop. We lived in Kazimierz, the Jewish quarter. The family was traditional but not

Orthodox. I had two sisters and two brothers. Like most Jewish boys, I began my schooling when I was three. First there was a Hebrew school, then elementary school, *gimnazium*, and finally university. At the same time I took violin and voice classes at the Kraków Conservatory. I never thought then that singing and even gymnastics would earn my bread in the future. I was very athletic and played tennis well but wanted to become an anthropologist. I was interested in prehistoric times and in philosophy. That was what I did my doctorate in. But I could not find work. However, there were jobs for physical education and singing teachers. I already had a family and I had to make some money, so I began teaching both subjects at the Hebrew *gimnazium* in Białystok. I moved there with my wife and two daughters in 1928."

"How many Jews were there in Białystok?"

"Fifty thousand. Half the population of the city."

"That was a large community."

"Large and wonderfully organized. We had a rich network of schools of the most widely assorted types; a multitude of religious, professional, charitable, cultural and sports organizations were active; numerous political parties..."

"You belonged to the Zionists."

"I did not so much belong as sympathize with them. That resulted from a long family tradition. Its consequence was the journey to Palestine of my parents and sisters in 1935."

"Why did you remain behind?"

"I felt needed here. I had links with Poland, with Polish Jews."

"The war found you in Białystok."

"As a result of the Ribbentrop-Molotov pact, the city was occupied by the Russians. Our *gimnazium* was converted on the Soviet model into a ten-grade school. Since the Russians did not acknowledge Hebrew, our language of instruction was changed to Yiddish and after a couple months more to Russian, ending our distinctiveness. Yet there was no time for grieving because before long the Soviet-German war broke out, and in June, 1941, the Germans entered Białystok. They confined the Jews to a ghetto almost immediately. They were to live there for two more years."

"You found yourself in the ghetto as well."

"Along with my family. In our ghetto the economic situation was not as tragic as in other cities. This resulted above all from the fact that we were not so isolated. The ghetto was surrounded only partly by a wall and partly by a wooden fence. So there was no hunger. We always had bread and potatoes."

"You belonged to a combat organization."

"For a long time there were conflicts within the ghetto over the method of fighting the Germans. Some people felt that the organization had to be created inside the ghetto, and others felt that all fighting in the ghetto was suicidal and that the only chance for even a partial victory lay in partisan warfare. Judyta Nowogrodzka led the latter. I belonged to her organization. Judyta was a communist, but the organization was generally not policital by nature. Furthermore, Judyta fell into conflict with her Party comrades, who wanted to remain in the ghetto.

"Thanks to the favorable situation many of our people managed to escape to the forest. I left the ghetto for the first time on May 23, 1943, along with a large group under my command. As a result of coincidences, however, we had to go back. Only when we returned to the ghetto did I realize that I was missing three people. So I went back, alone this time, to look for them. Beyond the wall I encountered a two-man German patrol. There was shooting, and I killed them both. That was my first such experience. It does not keep me awake nights, but I do not boast about it either, because I know that those two had someone waiting for them—a mother, a wife, children. I thought about it that way even then, despite the fact that we did not regard Germans as human beings, the same way they did not regard us as human beings. That night, however, I had no other choice. If I had not killed them, they would have killed me, and besides, the ghetto would have suffered for it under the system of collective responsibility."

"Afterward, you got away from the ghetto."

"Yes, after a few days I had no trouble. Later I was in the ghetto twice more. The last time was four days before its liquidation which began on August 16. Nobody expected anything in the ghetto; indeed, the atmosphere there was jubilant. In July, after the withdrawal of Italy from the Nazi coalition, there was even dancing in the streets. People believed in the approaching German defeat and rapid liberation."

"This was all taking place after the liquidation of the majority of the ghettos, after the destruction of millions of Jews. Didn't you know about that?"

"The ghettos were isolated. At first nobody knew anything. Then whispers about slaughters circulated. In the second half of 1942 there was more and more talk about Treblinka. The name was changed to Tremblinka because of what 'tremble' means in English. And in fact the very name made people tremble. Yet the reports were so incredible and so terrifying that people did not want to believe them. They simply did not want to know. That changed only at the end of the year. As a result of a German oversight, freight cars full of the possessions of Jews gassed at Treblinka were sent to us for unloading. Among the clothes, the people doing the work found documents belonging to inhabitants of the surroundings of Białystok—often their relatives, friends, and acquaintances. Only then did they believe. But at the same time came the victories of the Allies in North Africa and of the Russians at Stalingrad. Besides, apart from the handful who were organized, the people of the ghetto were completely defenseless. So they clung to every hope."

"And yet an uprising broke out during the liquidation."

"A group of young people, who had no chance at all, fought. They held out for three days. This is a bloody but shining page in one of the last chapters of the history of the Jews of Białystok."

"What were you doing at that time?"

"We were circling the whole time within a radius of eight or more miles around the ghetto, and we could not break through. Each of us had his family there. News of the destruction reached us very quickly. We were completely helpless. Twenty or thirty people, twenty or thirty pistols ... My wife and two daughters were being killed in the ghetto."

"What became of your unit?"

"After that horrible tragedy the previously dispersed groups were joined into one larger unit called Vorvoys, which means 'forward' in Yiddish. There were more than fifty of us. We went deep into the forest. We built a dugout there. The winter that year was exceptionally long, frozen, and severe. We survived thanks to the Polish population of the nearby village of Dworzysk. The peasants—and they all knew about us—not only did not turn us in but fed and helped us for many months. That winter we had two serious skirmishes with the Germans. Then, in the spring, we linked up with Soviet partisan units. My new unit was called Twenty-Six Years of October in honor of the Bolshevik revolution. The majority were Jews, although there were also Russians. About half of those Jewish partisans survived the war."

"Did you return to Białystok as soon as the Soviet army arrived?"

"Yes. I found a city that was free, but also free of Jews. Out of fifty thousand, there was a handful of us left. Several hundred more came later from the Soviet Union. It was necessary to create some sort of conditions in which these dispossessed, orphaned remnants could exist, and to assure them of help. A Jewish Committee was set up for Białystok and the whole region. I was chosen to be its leader in a democratic election. I filled that post for two years. In that period I met a Jewish woman, Edwarda Orłowska, and we were soon married. Edwarda was then the first secretary of the Party in town."

"Yet you did not join the Communist Party."

"I am not and never have been a communist."

"Not long afterward you undertook an unusual journey."

"I received news from my father in Palestine. He was summoning me. He was very ill and, as he wrote, he wanted to see his one surviving son before he died. I felt great respect for my father, and his will was a command to me. So I set out. It was a largely uncertain journey. I had a Polish passport with only one visa, for Czechoslovakia, in it. The English refused me a visa for Palestine. They were generally not giving them to Jews at the end of 1946. This was a continuation of their policy before and after the war. Yet if they had been admitted to Palestine, hundreds of thousands of Jews could have survived the time of destruction.

"Since I did not have a visa for Palestine, I could not obtain transit visas either, and starting from Austria, I sneaked across the open borders along with a group of illegal Jewish émigrés. This was the time of the great exodus. We crossed the Alps on foot and from Milan we reached Bari. In the port there we boarded an emigrant ship. It was called the *Patria*. As soon as we reached the open sea, we changed its name to the Hebrew *Moledet*, which means the same thing: fatherland. There were more than a thousand of us. Not far from the Palestinian coast we were stopped by the British navy, which was blockading the whole coast. The British ordered us to return. We did not obey, but we had to move back into the open sea. There the ship broke down. It was truly a wreck, and in addition it was significantly overloaded, so all the motors quit. We started drifting dangerously, and the captain sent out an SOS. Those same British ships rescued us. They put a line on the ship and towed it to Haifa, but only to reembark all of us on an English ship and deliver us to

Cyprus, to the camp in Karaolis. Several thousand Jews were interned there in conditions that were, by the standards of our wartime experience, altogether bearable. Next I was transferred to the camp in Xylokymlen. There I received a despairing letter from my father, begging me to come as soon as I could. He was in the hospital. It looked fatal. I went to the commander and outlined the problem. I asked him to let me go for a month, and I would give him my pledge to return on time. The commander answered that he understood, but there were regulations. To that I replied that I would try to escape, to which he replied that he would endeavor to prevent me. So it was a discussion between two gentlemen."

"And you did escape."

"I escaped in a sailboat, along with a young man from Silesia. The boat belonged to three Arabs. This was rather hazardous, since there were still anti-Jewish riots in Palestine at this time. I remember sitting alert, tense, in the stern, with my hand on a switchblade in my pocket. But these Arabs were professional ferrymen. They did not want to murder us, only to make some money. Unfortunately there was no wind just then, so we crossed the whole sea rowing in shifts. It took three days. The two of us were amazed at the ease with which we managed to land. There was not even a trace of the English ships, even though the blockade was still in force. Our ferryman sailed off at once, leaving us on a coastal road. In a moment a patrol appeared. We had nowhere to escape. Their uniforms seemed somewhat strange to us, but then we had never seen British infantry. I began speaking to them in English. They said nothing. So I asked, 'Where are we?' And I repeated: 'Palestine, Palestine.' They understood that and answered in French, 'No, this is Lebanon.' It all became clear. The ferrymen had wanted to make easy money, so they had delivered us where there was no blockade.

"The patrol escorted us to town, and we were taken before a court. These were Lebanese Christians. I pleaded the case for the defense in broken French. They let us off lightly: a month in prison. When we were released we traveled to Beirut. An illegal organization that smuggled Jews into Palestine contacted us there. Successful escapes from the camps in Cyprus were a rare occurrence, so our adventures were known everywhere. We were taken to the Palestine border in a luxury car. They gave us a guide, and we finally made it across the mountains to Erets. Altogether my journey had lasted eleven months."

"Was your father still alive?"

"Fortunately he lived several more years. His illness turned out to be not so serious. He was in the hospital in Bnei Brah. I spent several months with him there, and later at his home, until he had recovered fully. Then—and this was May, 1948—I returned by air to Poland."

"Why didn't you stay?"

"I had gone there to fulfill my obligations as a son. I had done homage to my father, but my wife was waiting for me in Warsaw. Besides, I had already decided long before to dedicate my life to research into the war crimes that the Germans had committed against the Jews. The best place for doing that was Poland. I returned and went to work at the Jewish Historical Institute. This lasted until 1953. It was a time of growing anti-Semitism in the Soviet Union. Provocations occurred in Moscow. The Jewish doctors who cared for Stalin were accused of wanting to poison him at the behest of the espionage organization called Joint. Today that sounds completely absurd. In those days it was dangerous indeed. My personal conflict revolved around the fact that the director of the Jewish Historical Institute, Bernard Mark, wrote anti-Joint interpolations into my article 'The Wehrmacht and Genocide.' This happened, of course, without my knowledge or consent, and in such a context it had unequivocal significance: recognition of the guilt of the 'criminals' and condemnation of their Jewish American backers. A sharp struggle broke out between the director and me. I wrote a letter protesting such procedures and categorically demanding a clarification. No clarification was forthcoming, and instead I was dismissed from work under Article 38 as an 'ideologically alien person.'"

"It was a short step from that article to prison."

"For me it ended in a mere blacklisting from intellectual employment, broadly understood. So I decided to become a mason. I took a course, passed an examination, and worked on various construction projects for two years. In 1955, when the turning away from Stalinism began, my professional banishment ended. I was able to go to work in the Central Commission for Research into Nazi Crimes. That was exactly what I was looking for. I had access to rich archives, and I could work in peace. I published a great deal. I also wrote a doctoral dissertation, and afterward the work that earned me the academic title *dozent*, or associate professor. So it went until 1968, a year that is not written with golden letters in the history of Poland. I had just reached retirement age, which became a good pretext to wave good-bye to me."

"You became director of the Jewish Historical Institute then."

"That lasted until 1970, when I retired for good. Of course, I have not given up scholarly work. Over the last fifteen years I have written a couple of books and several dozen articles."

"You have also prepared the first postwar Polish-language edition of selected talmudic texts."

"I am very pleased that the *Talmud* will finally come out in Polish."

"You are also a vice president of the Jewish Historical Institute, and your daughter Helena is carrying on the family tradition. She is a historian employed in the same institute, and she is writing a doctorate on Jewish assimilation in the nineteenth century."

"And I also have an eight-year-old granddaughter Ruth, my great treasure. Now you know everything about me."

"In a greatly condensed form."

"My dear, when you get to be eighty-three you have to recount your life in a condensed version because otherwise you would never finish."

"Now let's talk about Polish Jews. I want to begin by admitting something: I have been working on this book for many years, talking to a great many people, listening to their reminiscences, reading books, looking at old photographs. Despite this, I still cannot imagine the world of the Polish Jews that existed on this land such a short time ago. It seems as distant as the ancient Etruscans do from the present-day inhabitants of Rome. And yet we are not separated by millenia. Jews lived here, in the specific places that I have visited, barely forty-odd years ago. And yet in juxtaposition to what is here now, I simply cannot imagine it."

"Because it cannot be imagined—it must be experienced. The world of the Polish Jews was extraordinarily varied, rich, and colorful. And above all it was big and it was what I would call *present*: very visible. Jews made up ten percent of the population of the country, but since they lived predominantly in the towns, their numbers there were

proportionately much greater. In large cities, from 30 to 50%. In smaller towns, particularly in the eastern lands, the number of Jews ran as high as 80 or 90%. Those were the famous Jewish *shtetls.* And a splendid, exuberant, and creative Jewish life flourished everywhere in those towns and villages. There was complete freedom of observance and autonomy in religious matters, exceptionally well developed education of all types, at all levels, and in all specializations, as well as an enormous number of publications in all three languages: Yiddish, Hebrew, and Polish. Thirty Jewish newspapers and a hundred and thirty of the most varied magazines were being published just before the war. Literary giants, reformers, thinkers, scholars, and politicians grew up and worked in Poland. Dozens of political parties of all colorations were active. They had their delegates and senators in the Polish parliament. There were charitable and cultural organizations, unions of writers and journalists and workers. The *Talmud* blossomed within the Orthodox community. The world-famous Talmudic School was established in Lublin in 1930. Not long afterward the Judaic Institute, an important scholarly center occupied with research into the history and culture of the Jews as well as with gathering collections, was established in Warsaw. Thanks to all this, the Poland of those times was the world center of Jewish culture. Although they had been surpassed in quantitative terms by American Jews, Polish Jews remained far ahead in spiritual creativity."

Szymon Datner at home
with his one, beloved granddaughter, Ruth.

"But if it was so good, Mr. Datner, why was it so bad?"

"Are you thinking of anti-Semitism?"

"I am thinking of economic boycotts, ghetto benches, brawls. But of course the source of all this was anti-Semitism, for which Poland is famous to this day throughout the world."

"If we want to consider this problem seriously and to any degree impartially, which is extremely difficult, we must take a step backward. The history of the Jews in Poland covers a thousand years—exactly the same as the history of the country itself. Of course there is no adequate way to present Polish-Jewish relations in anything less than a thick book. But in order to frame the question honestly, it is necessary to say at least this much at the outset: Jews generally fared well in Poland. For long centuries, they lived significantly better here than in any other part of Europe or the world. That is also why the Jewish immigration to Poland was so large. Jews who had been persecuted, disinherited, tortured, and murdered elsewhere—and it should suffice to mention the period of the crusades or the unparalleled cruelty of fifteenth-century Spain—could find secure asylum in Poland. Poland was a country without pogroms; over the space of nine hundred years they can literally be counted on the fingers of one hand. If Jews were slaughtered, they died simultaneously with and like Poles, at the hands of foreign armies or rebellious Cossacks. As early as the thirteenth century the Jewish population in Poland was endowed with unusually liberal rights. The Jews possessed wide autonomy and were protected by law. The favorable legislation remained in force until the eighteenth century. Poland was forthrightly called a Jewish paradise. It is enough to mention that an independent Jewish parliament, called the Sejm of the Four Lands, operated in Lublin. Of course, this paradise was not entirely paradisical. There was strong antagonism against Jews on the part of the burghers, who were mainly of German extraction and had brought the concepts of hatred and extermination from there. Also, the attitude of the nobility exemplified the relationship of a capricious protector to an inferior, often slighted protégé. This situation prevailed until the fall of the Polish state and, with some modifications, until the twentieth century.

"A violent growth in nationalism throughout Europe characterized the turn of this century. Polish nationalism was further intensified by the struggle for the formation of a Polish state, and there was also Jewish nationalism. It was exactly at this point that Zionism arose and developed. This was hardly conducive to the harmonious cohabitation of two nations existing together. In addition, there was the negative influence of Russia, the partitioning power to which the greatest part of the former Polish lands belonged. Russia was traditionally anti-Semitic and the wave of pogroms after 1880 caused an influx of great numbers of Russian Jews into native Polish lands. And so, speaking with many abridgments and great simplification, we arrive at independent Poland—which means the twenty years between the wars."

"Three and a half million Jews then lived in Poland."

"And the forces of friction and hatred were great. There were several reasons. There is no doubt that great economic competition, in which Jews often prevailed, existed between Jews and Poles. This was true in heavy industry as well as among small producers, merchants, and craftsmen. These economic conflicts had ideological underpinnings. Here the greatest blame for inciting anti-Semitism lies with the National Democrats, the party that included extreme nationalism and fighting Jews in its program. The National Democrats had great influence, which grew with the deterioration of the economic situation—and these were the years of a great crisis that shook the economy of the whole world. On top of this there was the difference in faith, accented by both sides and all the more apparent because of the absolute freedom of religion. Unfortunately these sentiments were also fomented by Catholic priests."

"The Second Vatican Council was far in the future."

"Very far. Hatred was sown even from the pulpit. 'Jews crucified Christ' was the crowning argument."

"That claim sank so deeply into the popular awareness that it surfaces from time to time even now, and not only among the uneducated."

"That is really the worst thing. Certain schemas, stereotypes, and conceptual mixtures sink into the consciousness or the subconscious. Afterward they remain there, transferred, often unknowingly, from generation to generation. So it is in the mutual conceptions of Jews and Poles. Or in any case in the majority. Even Mickiewicz, the greatest Polish poet, wrote in *Pan Taceusz*, 'Like a child crippled by the needles of Jews.' That means that he believed that the Jews used the blood of Christian infants to make matzo. So even if Mickiewicz, who truly admired the Jews and often described them splendidly in his poems, believed such nonsense, what can we expect from others? From the indifferent or the hostile? The power of the stereotype is enormous, and in some cases it leads to catastrophic results."

"As it did in Poland, in 1939."

"The Second World War is a period that I have been dealing with for several decades, and I obstinately maintain that one must be very careful in passing judgment."

"But that is the period of Polish-Jewish relations that awakens the greatest controversies and passions."

"So let us try to discuss it calmly."

"In the West the problem of responsibility for the destruction is an eternally open question. Poles, too, are burdened with it. There exists a conviction,—at least in the lay consciousness—that Poles not only turned Jews over to the Germans en masse but also helped murder them."

"If we speak of moral responsibility, each individual must examine his conscience. Things are different, however, if we are talking about the responsibility for specific crimes. And the Holocaust was such a specific, though unimaginable, crime. But it cannot be charged against the Poles. It was German work and it was carried out by German hands. The Polish police were employed in a very marginal way, in what I would call keeping order. I must state with all decisiveness that more than 90% of that terrifying, murderous work was carried out by the Germans, with no Polish participation whatsoever."

"One of the main arguments of those who charge Poles with complicity in the Holocaust is the fact that the Germans created the largest extermination camps—Auschwitz, Treblinka, and others—here in

Poland. They say that this land was not chosen without good reason."

"The reason was and is very relevant: the largest concentration of Jews in Europe—greater, sometimes by an order of ten, than in other countries. The second reason is that the Poles, too, although at a slower tempo, were marked for extermination, and that in comparison with France or Holland, a ghastly terror prevailed in Poland. Such camps accorded well with the rest of the gloomy landscape here."

"But those who accuse Poles are not concerned with such answers."

"I know they are not, but such is the truth. Poles are not responsible for the crimes of the Holocaust. On the other hand, the Polish-Jewish problem in those days, if I can put it that way, lies in the approximately two hundred to two hundred fifty thousand Jews who tried to save themselves."

"How credible is that figure?"

"Not absolutely—like all figures concerning this problem. There was no way to make a precise count of the Jews who tried to save themselves. It was not even possible to establish how many were saved thanks to Poles, since many of these Jews left Poland immediately after the war. Among historians there is controversy over the number saved. The divergence is large: from fifty thousand according to Friedman to one hundred twenty thousand in the opinion of Kermisz from the Yad Vashem Institute in Jerusalem."

"What is your opinion?"

"My estimate, also intuitive to some degree, is that eighty to one hundred thousand were saved. In any case those Jews—approximately a quarter of a million people looking for help—were a problem for Poles. They tapped on the window of a cottage or the door of an apartment, and a question appeared alongside them: To save them or not? And how to do it? Would even a piece of bread help, or should I pretend not to hear anything? Or should I go and inform the Germans, which is what the law enjoins? Every form of aid was forbidden under pain of death for oneself and one's whole family."

"To us today the choice seems altogether clear. And yet I was shocked not long ago by a girl I know, a Jew. She is a person my age, someone I value highly for her honesty and courage. And she told me, 'I am not at all sure that I would give a bowl of food to a Pole if it could mean death for me and my daughter.'"

"It was a truly satanic moral trial that Poles were subjected to. I do not know if anyone else would have emerged victorious from it."

"But we didn't emerge either."

"My child, there is no answer to that ... On the other hand, to speak concretely of the attitude of Poles toward Jews: the majority of Poles behaved passively, but that can be explained by the terror and also by the fact that Poles, too, were being systematically murdered on a mass scale by the Germans. On the other hand, aside from passivity, which I regard as entirely justified by a situation in which every action was heroic, there also existed an indifference that I regard as negative—although even here one could look for a psychological explanation. Next, as if on parallel lines, come the two active groups. Those who betrayed, attacked, or murdered either from a desire for gain or out of pure hated, and those who sheltered Jews and aided them in various ways. The second group was more numerous and more representative both of Poles and of the leadership of the Polish underground. Yet the first group was more effective in its actions."

"What does that mean?"

"We sometimes forget that saving one Jew often took several or even a dozen or more people, with actions that generally lasted for long years. On the other hand, one person and one moment were enough to betray a Jew. Second, many attempts at aid ended in failure. Both the Jew and the Pole sheltering him died, and this is not counted in the positive statistics."

"It is often said that Polish help, especially that organized by the Home Army, came too late—only when the mass murders and the liquidation of the ghettos had begun, while earlier it might have been possible to save many more people."

"Many more people would, naturally, have been able to escape from the ghettos if they had known. But that is just the problem: in the ghettos they did not know, and when they found out they did not believe it. Neither did the Poles believe it, nor—despite the reports sent out from here—did anyone believe it abroad. It was impossible to believe that the nation of Goethe, Beethoven, and Heine had become a nation of murderers or that the state, whose task it is to protect citizens, would deliberately and methodically commit crimes against them. So no one believed it, and of course that was a mistake."

"So it would have been possible to do more."

"It is always possible to do more. A book called *The Abandonment of the Jews* was recently published in the U.S. This is a scholarly treatment demonstrating the indifference of America and its principal ally Great Britain to the destruction of millions of European Jews. The author, a history professor, presents the inertia of governments, institutions, and individuals. He makes use of facts, evidence, and documents. Rarely does he allow himself to make comments. The book concludes with a list of actions that could have been undertaken. This book shocked many Americans. 'We were not our brothers' keepers and we must bear the burden of shame for our indifference,' wrote the historian Frank Freidel after reading it. So it is. Everyone could have done more. Much more."

"So why are Poles above all remembered for their bad deeds, while the good ones are forgotten?"

"Because wrongs are carved in stone and good deeds in sand."

"That is not fair."

"No, my child, it is not. But it fits the human spirit, which reacts violently to wrong and cherishes the memory of it."

"But what is your opinion? Do you think that Poles generally behaved properly?"

"I do not think so. But as to the question, according to whom should the nation be judged—by those who denounced or by those who saved lives—I have no doubts."

"So let us pass on to the immediate postwar period. For me personally this is the most painful period of Polish-Jewish relations. After the way three million Poles and three million Polish Jews had died on this land, instead of final reconciliation there was an explosion of negative emotions."

"Yes, that is a tragic chapter, and furthermore one that has been studied very little. For more than two years a fratricidal war went on in which one murdered the other. Jews, however, were murdered with particular persistence."

"Why?"

"Mostly, I think, because they took the side of the new authorities in the overwhelming majority."

"Regardless of conviction?"

"There exists such a thing as Jewish legalism. This means a great loyalty to the authorities, and particularly to authorities that guarantee the safety of the Jews. So it was in this case. In official documents, the communist government assured the Jews of equal rights, compensation for damages, and assistance in rebuilding their existence."

"While Poles came out in the overwhelming majority against the new authorities that had been imposed on them against their will."

"Yes, that stirred up resentment."

"As did the large number of Jews among the communist cadres."

"Those for whom Poland had been a Jewish world found only cemeteries there after the war. The main argument for staying was therefore sympathy for the system, because otherwise it would be better to go to Palestine or the U.S. Most of all it was those who sympathized with communism that stayed."

"When I talk about Polish-Jewish problems, these two themes

come up in every conversation. The Jews say: anti-Semitism. The Poles: Commie Jew."

"This generalizing from individual cases is truly unfortunate. You cannot say Poles are anti-Semites or Jews are communists. Both Poles and Jews are individual people, and we have to treat each other as individual people."

"I would certainly not want to have to prove to every Jew I meet that I am not an anti-Semite. And yet Jews, who treat everyone who isn't an anti-Semite as an exception, constantly demand exactly such assurances and proofs from Poles."

"Or else they immediately classify that exception as a philo-Semite."

"I always repeat, 'I am neither a philo-Semite nor an anti-Semite. I am normal.' But they do not believe me."

"My dear, you see yourself how difficult it is, and you belong to the generation born after the war. So think of the force of emotions connected with those matters forty years ago. Poles were traditionally anticommunist, both before the war and after its conclusion. Against that background the proportionally large presence of Jews in the prewar Communist Party of Poland was very visible. Many of these Jewish communists escaped to the USSR. After 1944 they returned to hold high offices in the Polish government, Party, and army."

"Some regard this as a deliberate tactic of Stalin's—placing Jews in exposed and particularly hated positions, for instance, in the security apparatus."

"Perhaps, although from the Polish point of view that was not significant. It is a fact that the presence of Jews and the functions they executed seemed fully to confirm the slogans about 'Commie Jews.' The effect was tragic. The growth of anti-Semitism, and a rapacious murderous anti-Semitism at that. What is worse, the victims were predominantly entirely innocent people. I remember such incidents from that period, when I was the head of the Jewish Committee in Białystok. In February, 1945, six Jews who had returned there were murdered in the town of Sokoły. Among them was a little girl, Tola. To this day I have photographs of the corpses. I went there alone and brought the bodies to Białystok, where we buried them. I delivered the eulogy at the cemetery."

"What did you say?"

"Exactly what I said earlier—that the Polish people were not to blame for what had happened, since it was the work of individuals. And that they should pay the penalty."

"Did they pay?"

"It seems to me that they did. The Polish authorities were not indulgent toward the murderers."

"The murdering of Jews returning to small towns had, it seems to me, one more basis. Jews were returning to their houses, stores, and workshops. Yet these already had new owners who did not like the idea of giving them back. Although, of course, not everyone was prepared to murder for this reason."

"Yes, anti-Semitism also fed on such petty interests. One more problem was equally important. During the five years of the war, the life of a Jew had been worth nothing, and human life as such had grown cheap. And now, after the war, it was rather easy to kill each other. You might call it a general brutalization."

"How many Jews were killed after the war?"

"In the first year, according to the data of the Jewish Central Committee, 353 people."

"And afterward?"

"At least twice as many more. In the Kielce pogrom alone, forty-two people died. Accusations of ritual murder by Jews served as the pretext."

"It has never been possible to research this matter thoroughly, but the majority of historians regard that incident as having been instigated by the government."

"It is certainly true that the municipal authorities demonstrated complete neutrality and inaction. Order was restored only after troops were brought in from elsewhere."

"After the Kielce pogrom, during the funeral of the three *Chalutzim* murdered in Białystok, you again delivered a eulogy. This time, however, you called on Jews to leave Poland."

"I said then that the price for staying in Poland was too high."

"In this period emigration from Poland, legal and illegal, increased greatly."

"In the course of the year after the Kielce pogrom, a hundred thousand Jews emigrated. And from then until 1950 at least fifty thousand more."

"How many Jews remained?"

"The data of the Jewish Central Committee from July 1946, or just before the Kielce pogrom, show more than two hundred forty thousand. That was the result of reimmigration from the USSR. Then those one hundred fifty thousand left. And exactly how many remained it is hard to say. In any case, the successive emigrations of 1956 and 1968 left Poland almost without Jews. A handful remained, a couple of thousand people."

"There are almost no Jews. And what about anti-Semitism?"

"The problem lies first of all in the fact that Poles have not settled their own accounts. That abscess has not been publicly lanced."

"I agree, except that there is no way of publicly taking up this problem in an honest way. I have experienced this myself, when the censor brutally cut all my texts about Jews or Polish-Jewish relations."

"That is true. Yet as long as we do not write about this subject forthrightly and openly—as long as the view that Poles are good to Jews but Jews are ungrateful prevails in official pronouncements and individual consciousnesses—Poland will not enjoy credibility on this issue."

"What does the tiny Jewish community in Poland look like at the present time?"

"They are predominantly old people. The average age is seventy. Most of them are alone and require protection and assistance. So it is necessary to do anything to alleviate their suffering. This is exactly what we deal with, aside from religious functions, in the Congregation of the Mosaic Faith. Joint plays a large role here, giving material aid to nearly all the Jews in Poland and additionally supplying canned kosher food to our cafeterias. Joint also helps those Poles who saved Jews during the war and now, themselves mostly elderly, find themselves in difficult circumstances. I also know that many of the Jews who were saved maintain warm contacts with their saviors, and in the Grove of the Righteous near the Yad Vashem Institute in Jerusalem nearly half of the trees have been planted by Polish hands."

"An enormous number of Jewish monuments existed on Polish land. What has happened to them?"

"The majority have collapsed. During the war the Germans destroyed synagogues and their furnishings methodically, and they stole valuables. After the war emigrating Jews took a great deal of the remaining Judaica with them. This covers, above all, Scriptural scrolls, old books, and also cult objects. Part of what is left is in museums and part is in private hands. And it is often lost. Especially books. These collections, not so much hidden as put aside or mislaid, are in a condition of complete neglect. From time to time a volume sees the light of day when it is uncovered and offered for sale by an owner who needs money."

"If we are talking about books, though, I think the big problem is a lack of knowledge of Hebrew. I've heard about book collections in state libraries that have been crated up for decades, for the simple reason that no one knows how to deal with them."

"There is a Hebrew Studium at the University of Warsaw, but it does not seem to be top level. In any case, the graduates of the Studium are not prepared to immerse themselves in old Jewish folios."

"How many people in Poland know Hebrew at present?"

"There is Professor Friedman, there is me, there might be

somebody else ..."

"And what is happening with the architectural monuments?"

"Some of the surviving synagogues have been restored. They are no longer places of worship, however, because there is no one left who could pray in them. Some of the monuments are deteriorating, falling down. Even here some work is being done, but it demands billions of złoty. And now we are not talking about intentions but about capabilities. Poland is in a severe economic crisis. It is a poor country. There is not even enough money to save Wawel Castle, which is the most valuable national monument that the Poles have. So there is no thought of funding for other similar goals."

"And cemeteries? There are more than four hundred fifty of them in Poland and most of them are in disastrous shape."

"This is a very painful problem. The Germans destroyed most of the cemeteries, either demolishing them on the spot or ordering that the stones be used for paving the streets. Jews themselves often had to do this. After the war, therefore, we found our cemeteries in very poor shape. Only a few places, like the Remu Cemetery could be put in order. Afterward, the Jews left, and the cemeteries were completely abandoned. They are formally under the management of the Congregation. But how can we, a few old people, go about caring for several hundred cemeteries scattered all over the country? So they go on collapsing."

"It is thought, particularly abroad, that Poles deliberately destroy Jewish cemetaries."

"They are a no man's land. Sheep and cows graze there, the local drunks go there to imbibe, and someone occasionally breaks a tombstone. But these are outbreaks of hooliganism rather than symptoms of a dislike for Jews."

"And digging up graves to look for valuables?"

"There are cemetery hyenas everywhere, and they usually gorge themselves in unguarded places."

"For a couple of years, a Social Committee for the Protection of Jewish Cemeteries has been active in Poland."

"People, especially the young, are trying to do something, and I praise them for that. Except that this is a job for thousands, and it demands enormous funding that is not there."

"Mr. Datner, during my conversations with Polish Jews one issue always surfaces: fear. It is imbedded, more or less concealed, in everyone, regardless of age, background, or present circumstances."

"In this matter I cannot link myself with my brethren. There is no fear in me. Perhaps that is because I am already old. The fact that I will soon have to take my leave is a source of peace for me."

"How do you see the future of Polish Jews? Is there any future at all?"

"Polish Jews give the impression of a group that is becoming extinct. But after all, our people have been dying for two thousand years and somehow they have not died out. Of course, this community in Poland has been reduced. But it can survive. New, young people came to us not long ago. It seemed that they had fallen away from the Jewish tree, and yet they have returned. Three months ago I experienced great joy—

there was a *Bar Mitzvah.* So, perhaps, there will be something, someone left, when we are gone … And besides, I am generally an optimist. Take a look around: the Polish Jews were cut down to the stump, but the powerful Jewry of America has grown. Now there are six million of them—as many as were murdered in Europe. The state of Israel was established, and new generations of Jews have grown up there. Yes, even if some branches are cut off, and if others wither and fall, the Jewish people exist and will exist."

Pope John Pa
at the Heroes of the Ghetto Monument in Wa
during his second pilgrimage to Pol
The Pope visited the monument on his own initia
outside his official government itine
This symbolized for Poles and Jews alike the Pope's d
for reconciliation between the two gro

Seder at the Warsaw Jewish community.
"We are making our exit; we will be gone in a moment."
This statement was often repeated during my talks
with Polish Jews.

as raised
completely assimilated family
I knew literally nothing
ut Jews, their culture, and tradition,"
Izaak Walczak. Now
lways wears the Star of David.

Glossary of Hebrew and Yiddish Terms

Aron Kodesh— receptacle in the synagogue in which the *Torah* scrolls are kept.

badchen— entertainer, especially at Jewish weddings in Eastern Europe.

Bar Mitzvah— ceremony in which a boy enters into the Jewish religious community as a responsible adult. It takes place in the synagogue, usually on the first Sabbath after the boy's thirteenth birthday. The boy is then called on to read the *Torah* in public for the first time.

beit midrash— school with its own library of rabbinical works where students gather for study, discussion, and prayer under the direction of rabbinic teachers.

bimah— dais or platform in the synagogue upon which a reading desk is placed and from which the *Torah* is read.

cantor— principal leader of the prayers in the synagogue. Since the prayers are sung, the ideal cantor is described as pious, mature, scholarly, and possessed of a mellifluous voice.

challah— the loaf of bread baked especially for the Sabbath.

Chalutzim— pioneers, especially farmers, in Israel.

Chassidism— mystical, religious and social movement founded by Israel ben Eliezer (c. 1700–1760), known as Baal Shem Tov, in eastern Poland. Chassidism, which was opposed by the more orthodox rabbis and communal leaders, proclaimed that purity of heart was superior to study. Devotion to God was shown through religious ecstasy, dance, and song. Chassidism developed its own religious ritual, founded its own synagogues, but never entirely broke from rabbinical Judaism. Eastern Europe and particularly Poland were the centers of Chassidism before the Second World War; its current centers are in Israel and the United States.

cheder— religious school for children from three to thirteen. The *Torah* and the *Talmud* are studied.

chuppah— the portable canopy under which the Jewish wedding ceremony is held.

gaon— in common Yiddish usage, a brilliant man, a genius.

goy— non-Jew; gentile; one who is ignorant of Jewish customs.

Haggadah—extensive body of literature which varies considerably in content and form and includes biblical interpretations, old legends, moral sayings, prophetic admonitions, etc. The Passover *Haggadah*, a book from the Aggadic tradition, contains the service of the *seder* for the home and consists in large part of the narrative of the Exodus from Egypt.

Haskalah—the movement (c. 1750–1880) for spreading modern European culture among Jews in order to enable them to achieve equality. Its adherents supported intellectual and social conformity with the non-Jewish world, and modernization and westernization of Jewish religion and customs. Orthodoxy opposed the *Haskalah*.

Kabbala—the mystical religious stream in Judaism.

kaddish—traditional prayer that has become associated with mourners as a prayer for the dead.

Kehilla—an organized Jewish community or congregation.

kosher—food permitted and prepared according to Jewish dietary law which prohibits the eating of certain animals and the mixing of meat with milk products. Animals, to be considered kosher, must be slaughtered according to specific regulations.

koyen—a descendant of the ancient priests accorded certain privileges and obligations by Jewish law. *Koyenim* are subject to strict laws of purity regarding, among other things, contamination by corpses and the choice of a wife.

matzevah—monument, usually a gravestone.

mechuts—outside of the mainstream.

mensch—mature or responsible person.

mezuzah—a small parchment scroll inscribed with the biblical verses, Deut. VI 4–9 and XI 13–21. The scroll is placed in a small, often decorative case which is nailed to the doorframe of the Jewish home.

midrash—biblical commentaries in story form.

minyan—a group of ten adult male Jews, the minimum required for communal prayer. A young man who has had his *Bar Mitzvah* is an adult and may be counted in the minyan. Virtually all modern Reform congregations and many Conservative congregations also count adult women in the *minyan*.

mohel—religious functionary who performs the rites of circumcision according to rabbinic regulation.

Pesach— Passover. Seven-day spring festival (eight days outside Israel) commemorating the exodus of the Israelites from Egypt, and marking the barley harvest. As it is prohibited to use leaven during the festival, only unleavened bread (matzo) is eaten. The first night (and the second, outside Israel) is marked by a service with a meal in the home, the seder, during which the *Haggadah* is read and ritually prescribed foods are eaten.

Purim— holiday commemorating the saving of the Jews in Persia from the intended persecutions of Haman, minister to King Ahashuerus. On *Purim*, the Book of Esther, which describes these events, is read. It is a holiday of joy during which family and friends exchange gifts and hold feasts and performances. *Purim* is called the "Jewish carnival."

Rosh Hashanah— Two-day holiday commencing the Ten Days of Penitence which end on the Day of Atonement. Termed the "New Year," traditionally it is the day marking the Creation of the world, as well as the Day of Judgement when the fate of each person for the coming year is inscribed in the Book of Life. The religious ritual for the day features the blowing of the *shofar*, a ram's horn.

seder— ceremony observed in Jewish homes on the first night of Passover. The *Haggadah* is read and certain symbolic foods are eaten.

Shabbat— (Ashkenazic and Yiddish pronunciation, "*Shabbes*") the day of rest, observed from shortly before sunset on Friday to nightfall on Saturday. The day is marked by rest from labor, special synagogue services, study, and a family meal.

shabbes goy— a non-Jew hired on the Sabbath by Jews to perform any tasks that are prohibited to Jews on that day.

shammes— a synagogue sexton. The term is also used to denote the additional candle used in kindling the *Channukah* lights.

Shavuot— festival which occurs seven weeks after Passover and commemorates the giving of the *Torah* on Mount Sinai. Originally a festival of the first crops of wheat and fruits.

shaygets— (pl. *shkotsim*) a gentile boy; also, a scoundrel, smart-aleck.

shochet— slaughterer who follows the correct ritual for preparation of kosher meat.

shtetl— Jewish small town or village in Eastern Europe.

Simchat Torah— holiday marking the annual completion of the cycle of *Torah* readings in the synagogue. The *Torah* scrolls are taken out of the ark and carried around the synagogue seven or more times with singing and often dancing.

Succoth— festival of the harvest occurring in autumn, five days after *Yom Kippur.* During the festival, religious Jews dwell, or at least eat meals, in the *sukkah,* an outdoor booth decorated with harvest fruits and holiday symbols.

tallis— prayer shawl worn by adult males. Usually made of wool, it is a rectangular piece of fabric with biblically prescribed fringes in the corners.

tallis katon— smaller type of *tallis* worn under the outer clothing by Orthodox males.

Talmud— name given to two great collections which contain records of the wide-ranging discussions of generations of scholars. Subjects include religious, philosophic, ethical, civil, and secular matters.

tefilin— two leather boxes attached to leather straps which are bound onto the arm and head by adult male Jews during weekday morning prayer.

Torah— the first five books of the Bible, known as the "Written Law." Also, in the broader sense, both the Written and the Oral Law, the oral exposition of *Torah* traditionally traced back to Moses. The scroll of law used in the synagogue is referred to as the *Torah.*

trayf— unclean, not kosher.

tzaddick— a person known for outstanding piety. The Chassidim attached special significance to *tzaddikim* whom they regarded as miracle workers. Eventually, in the Chassidic world, the role of the *tzaddik* became hereditary.

Yahweh— conjectured pronunciation for the ineffable name of the God of Israel.

yarmulka— skull cap worn by males for prayers, and by traditional Jews at all times.

Yeshiva— higher Jewish school devoted primarily to the study of the *Talmud* and rabbinic literature.

Yom Kippur— the Day of Atonement. Solemn day of repentance and fasting. On this day many Jews who never go to the synagogue during the rest of the year attend the *Yizkor* service to honor departed relatives.

Chronology of Major Events in Polish-Jewish History

1096— Arrival in Poland of Jews escaping persecutions at the time of the first Crusade.

1264— Privileges granted to Jews by Duke Bolesław of Kalusz.

1334— King Casmir the Great expands the privileges of 1264.

1349— Massacre of Jews during the Black Death in Europe brings more Jews to Poland.

1399— First blood libel trial and persecution in Poznan.

1454— King Casmir the Jagiellonian repeals Jewish privileges.

1495— Jews are expelled from Kraków and settle in nearby Kazimierz; Jews expelled from Lithuania, reintroduced 1508.

1551— Charter of King Sigismund Augustus gives the Jewish communal leadership broad powers.

1500s— Center of Talmudic studies moves to Poland (Salomon Luria in Lublin, Moses Isserles in Kraków's Kazimierz).

1581–1764— Council of Four Lands, consisting of representatives of Jewish communities from Poland and Lithuania, exercises Jewish autonomy and collects taxes from Jews.

1648— Cossak uprising under Chmielnitsky in Polish Ukraine results in widespread massacre of Jews.

1700— Israel Baal Shem Tov, founder of the Chassidic movement, born in Okopy.

1755–1791— Growth of Jacob Frank's messianic sect; hundreds of his followers convert to Catholicism, obtaining nobility status.

1700s— Rise and development of Chassidic movement conflicts with the rabbinic establishment headed by Elijah, the Gaon of Vilna.

1794— Berek Joselewicz's Jewish regiment participates in the Polish Kosciusko insurrection against invading Russian armies.

1795— Poland is partitioned by Russia, Prussia, and Austria.

1807— Constitution of the Duchy of Warsaw grants equal rights to the Jews.

1861— Patriotic anti-Russian manifestos by Poles and Jews.

1881— First pogrom in Warsaw, condemned by Church and intellectuals.

1881–1924— Peak of Jewish emigration to the United States.

1905— Jewish workers' mass participation in the revolutionary movement.

1918— Poland regains independence; pogrom in Lwów takes place in the wake of Polish-Ukrainian struggle for the city.

1919— Poland signs Versailles treaty of minority rights; Jews elected to Polish parliament.

1921— Polish constitution grants equal rights to the Jews.

1919–1939— Jewish religious, cultural, and political life flourishes in Poland; many Jews assimilate to Polish culture, but face hostility that makes their integration difficult.

1935–1937— Pogroms testify to the rise of anti-Semitism.

1936— Prime Minister supports economic boycott of Jews.

1938— Polish Jews living in Germany brutally expelled.

1939— Poland partitioned by Germany and Russia.

1940— Jews in Warsaw confined to specially-created ghetto.

1941— Massacre of Jews by Germany begins in eastern Poland.

1942— German extermination camps become fully operational; destruction of Warsaw ghetto; Polish resistance movement gathers strength.

1943— Warsaw Ghetto uprising.

1945— More than 90% of Polish Jews perish; Poland liberated, Communist regime installed.

1946— Kielce pogrom; mass emigration of Jews.

1948— Poland becomes one of the first states to recognize Israel.

1949— Zionist organizations dissolved.

1957— Following liberalization, new mass emigration of Jews.

1967— After Six-Days War, Poland breaks off diplomatic relations with Israel.

1968— Government-sponsored campaign of anti-Semitism; final emigration of Jews.

1981— Reappearance of anti-Semitism, condemned by Solidarity, Church, and intellectuals.